Praise for *Quick Confidence*

"The perfect clapback to the ultimate existential crisis of not feeling enough. This is a beautifully written manual for the self on how to get there from here when it seems too far and too hard."

—**Margaret Cho,**
Comedian and actor

"This book delivers an instant injection of inspiration. Writing with both wit and compassion, Rezvani shows how to stop playing it safe and live a life of greater boldness. Whether making meaningful first impressions, pitching your next big idea, or staying resilient in the face of rejection, *Quick Confidence* is insight, persona, and best of all, actionable."

—**Daniel H. Pink,**
#1 *New York Times* bestselling author of
The Power of Regret, Drive, and *To Sell is Human*

"If you want to move, speak or think with more confidence, this is the book for you. Selena Rezvani masterfully distills the most essential confidence-building habits, so you can go after your biggest, boldest goals."

—**Jason Feifer,**
Editor-in-Chief, *Entrepreneur* magazine

"By the time you finish Selena Rezvani's book, you'll have kicked your limiting beliefs to the curb. Her stories are relatable, her tips are relevant and fresh – you'll be inspired to believe in yourself more and to keep reaching higher."

—**Coby Miller,**
2x U.S. Olympian and Medalist, Track and Field

". . .A powerful, thought-provoking book about how we can develop self-belief in our careers and beyond."

—**Mika Brzezinski,**
"Morning Joe" co-host and Know Your Value founder

"If you want to feel unstoppable and supremely inspired, read this book. Selena Rezvani shows us how to conquer the moments that matter most by multiplying self-belief—one action at a time."

—**Ann Anaya,**
SVP and Chief Diversity, Equity, and Inclusion Officer,
AmerisourceBergen

"To be a force for good in your career, you need the confidence to express your thoughts, share your ideas, and admit to mistakes. Selena Rezvani's *Quick Confidence* teaches us how to nurture self-confidence, no matter how high the stakes. Substantive and practical, this book will help you inspire confidence in those around you as well—to empower them to use their voices, take courageous risks, and challenge the status quo."

—Amy C. Edmondson, PhD,
Harvard Business School Professor, author
of *The Fearless Organization*,
and Thinkers50 #1 Ranked Management Thinker

"Whether you're navigating a new career move or regaining your footing after a setback, Selena Rezvani's *Quick Confidence* is the manual we all need to take fearless action. Delivered through powerful and practical tips and stories, Selena lowers the hurdles to help each of us speak up, show up, and lead."

—Anna Ransley,
Chief Information Officer, Godiva Chocolatier

"*Quick Confidence* is a practical guide for building and practicing self-confidence daily. Filled with small, doable actions, this book will give you the courage to follow your passions and embrace your joy!"

—Jen Fisher,
Chief Well-being Officer, Deloitte

QUICK
confidence

QUICK
confidence

Be Authentic,
Boost Connections, and Make
Bold Bets on Yourself

Selena Rezvani

WILEY

Library of Congress Cataloging-in-Publication Data

Names: Rezvani, Selena, author.
Title: Quick confidence : be authentic, boost connections, and make bold
    bets on yourself / Selena Rezvani.
Description: Hoboken, New Jersey : John Wiley & Sons, Inc. [2023] |
    Includes bibliographical references and index.
Identifiers: LCCN 2022057621 (print) | LCCN 2022057622 (ebook) | ISBN
    9781394160945 (hardback) | ISBN 9781394160969 (adobe pdf) | ISBN
    9781394160952 (epub)
Subjects: LCSH: Self-confidence. | Interpersonal relations. | Success.
Classification: LCC BF575.S39 R498 2023 (print) | LCC BF575.S39 (ebook) |
    DDC 158.1—dc23/eng/20230303
LC record available at https://lccn.loc.gov/2022057621
LC ebook record available at https://lccn.loc.gov/2022057622

Cover Design: Wiley
Cover Image: © Shtonado/Shutterstock
Author photo: © Gabrielle Smarr

SKY10044627_032223

This book is dedicated to anyone who's ever struggled to feel like "enough," who said yes when they meant no, who talked themselves out of an exciting dream, or who quaked at the thought of taking that first step.

This book also goes out to anyone who's ever felt like throwing traditional confidence books out a fourth-floor window. A big part of the confidence journey just can't be faked. I hope that every bit of information in this book brings you closer to who you are and that it helps you change your story and change your life.

CONTENTS

INTRODUCTION

When good things happen, do you ever walk around thinking the bottom could fall out at any minute? Like you're just waiting for things to *decline*?

I regularly counsel my coaching clients *not* to do this, but a few years ago that exact thing happened to me.

At 42, I was practically pumping my fist, overjoyed at a record year in my speaking and coaching business. All the late nights writing articles and books, prepping speeches, and hiring a kickass team seemed to be paying off. Not far in my memory were the early days of my business, when I was knocking on doors and actually begging clients to work with me. Now, not only were my clients exciting, certified cool companies, *they were coming to me*! Whoa.

I steeled myself for a big year to come and felt reassured that my young twins were now school-aged. They were doing well and becoming more self-sufficient by the day. *This* is what people must mean when they say, "I'm in a groove!"

Then, the world changed—overnight.

As the pandemic erupted, things like our health, safety, and level of contact became *the only things*. It's what occupied more of our thoughts and well—it's what mattered. Just like lots of people, I worried about the future. I felt helpless. I was fearful about susceptible relatives and loved ones. Adjusting to homeschooling two kids while schools were closed was another startling change.

Ugh! So much for that groove.

But as it became clear the pandemic wasn't going to be a short-lived blip, my business took a hard left turn. Company after company cancelled their events with me, cited unforeseen event clauses in their contracts, and pulled out of negotiations. Talk about a gut punch. As I watched all that hard-won security fall away, I realized how close my self-confidence was to falling away with it. Without this lineup of clientele, what exactly did I have to stand on? At that moment, when everyone was asking, "How will you pivot?" I had no idea, I just knew I didn't feel I had "the answer."

Not just that, but in the weekly chats I was having with my girlfriends, successful women directing important work at some of the largest companies in the United States, I noticed a stark change in their tone. Dubbed The Momrades (mom+comrades, get it?), our group was full of women who you could describe as ambitious, assured, buoyant. Now, though? They felt deeply uncertain, like their employers could lay them off or "re-org" them at any moment. They were understandably trying to get the temperature on things, keeping their heads down, and playing it safer at work. Add to this a raw, pervasive sense of burnout—as one friend put it, "We're trying to solve all the old problems in our jobs, but we have even more new ones."

As I put my ear to the buzz in my online communities, I heard *the exact same sentiment.* People were negotiating job stress, new financial worries, health and bodily concerns, cancelled childcare, and more.

For so many workers, their sense of agency and self-confidence was at the curb. Speaking for myself, I felt side-swiped by a queasy mix of fear, uncertainty, and loss. Can you relate? Somehow I'm betting yes.

And that's when I realized something.

What if I could lessen the scariness and uncertainty of this time, even a tad, and give people a little, tiny fortifier? What if, in shoring up my own bleeding self-confidence, I could also help other people build up theirs? Bit by bit?

On one hand, I had this strong feeling people were really hungry for more confidence in their lives (I know I was!). But I questioned if it would add value—if it made "business sense" or if it was "too fluffy." And I wondered if something like a newsletter was a good idea or a passing impulse.

But the next day, before I lost my moxie, I typed LinkedIn into my browser and hit "Create a newsletter." I decided I'd call it *Quick Confidence.* (Not only do I love the topic of self-confidence, but I knew if I wanted to make a promise I could make good on, it would be keeping things brief!) Besides, most of us don't have loads of spare time for a confidence intensive. We need actionable, memorable tips we can apply on the go.

I made a colorful header on my laptop and uploaded it. I decided each issue would address a specific facet of building confidence—things such as dealing with intimidating people, getting ready for a high-stakes moment, asking for a flexible arrangement, rebuilding your confidence after a setback, and many more. To add variety, rather than offering people three general tips in each letter, I separated them into embodied tips, mindset tips, and interpersonal tips and provided one of each in every issue.

Gulp. Here we go.

I sent out the first one, promising to make it a weekly thing—and something amazing began to happen.

People read it. They commented on it. And so many of them shared it! And soon it had thousands of subscribers. With each issue I wrote, I felt *myself* gaining little confidence wins, ingesting and absorbing the same messages I was asking others to internalize. New clients materialized too, saying, "I found you through your newsletter!"

And people's success stories? They are like jet fuel to me.

"I used the trick you taught on rebalancing power, and it really helped with my executive presentation."

"I did what you suggested in terms of confident body posture, and I felt more cool and assured networking last night."

"I decided to stop breaking promises to myself all the time, and it's helping."

Each comment hammered home that this confidence stuff is not inconsequential—or merely fluff!—in our lives.

Fast-forward to today, my newsletter is 90,000 subscribers strong and counting. I no longer see it as a letter—but a *forum*, a practice, a gathering place and source of encouragement for people all over the world. And did I mention that the best part of my week is reading people's comments, questions, and experiences? The icing on the cake came when LinkedIn recognized the newsletter as one of the best in the LinkedIn ecosystem.

That's why pitching a book on confidence felt like a natural extension of the newsletter momentum. How cool would it be to curate all the different tips, grouping them to address common challenges—that we all face? So people could make bold bets on themselves—and do big things? I set about doing just that.

Those four sentences make it sound easy, don't they? It wasn't. Forever humbled that I am a student *and* a teacher, I faced at least a dozen publisher rejections (ouch!) before getting my "Yes." In fact, pitching this book—the very one in your hands—was a culminating lesson in all the confidence tips I'd spent over a year writing and sharing.

So, what's the point of sharing the flash, the flicker, that started this confidence movement? What's the takeaway?

I could write a book of the lessons I've learned on this confidence journey—*oh wait*. But joking aside, I think my biggest, most inspiring and confidence-boosting takeaway from my idea-to-newsletter-to-book experience is this: Often we discount an aspiration as a silly urge or passing impulse. Even if it sparks joy or fills us with energy, we tell ourselves all the reasons it could go wrong. We forget about the central idea—the fire—that got us excited in the first place.

Well, I'm here to tell you those sparks are *worth paying attention to*. This book is proof of it!

To recognize the fire of your best ideas, you need to *practice* self-confidence. As you do, you'll become more attuned to ideas when they bubble up and, importantly, you'll have more of the motivation needed to execute them.

Together in this book, we'll tackle small, doable actions you can take to build lasting self-confidence. That's going to help you make strong first impressions *right out of the gate*. That way, you build new relationships on strong footing. We'll look at how to create self-belonging too, even when the people or conditions around you don't foster or encourage it.

We'll explore managing power—harnessing your own power when you're diminished or talked over and resisting the urge to overemphasize *others' power*. That's important particularly if you find yourself in a toxic culture or surrounded by toxic people—you'll learn tips for those sticky scenarios too.

Part of this confidence journey means subtracting—letting go of overdoing, overthinking, and overanalyzing. Can't all of us commit to doing that here and there? Maybe more often than that! Letting go sets you up to rise to the occasion in those especially big, career-making moments, freeing you to really focus on your best gifts and talents.

Together, we'll also look at how to negotiate your needs so people listen, and so you can get the green light or "yes" answer you need. As you use these tips to manage even those unavoidable fails and setbacks, I hope you'll highlight the table of contents, dog-ear the book, mark it, and bookmark it—to bring you right to the tip you need in a given moment.

We'll even explore how to scale your confidence, incorporating tips that help you multiply and accelerate your practice of developing healthy self-respect and appreciation over time. And maybe even pass it on to someone else who really needs it.

To help you, each tip in this book is meant to support you with the physical, mental, and interpersonal aspects of building confidence. Now these are not always hard-and-fast categories—some overlap and intersect at times. For example, coming up with a ritual to let go of a tough rejection might be part physical, part mental. But the categories matter because they help us to use *all of our faculties*—to divvy up the work of confidence in a sense and give homework to a specific part of ourselves. I've found that wildly effective in building self-confidence, and I think you will too. The tips focus on:

- Mindset—belief systems, attitudes, dispositions, ways of thinking

- Embodied—body language, tangible expressions, mannerisms, movements, physical responses

- Interpersonal—relationship behaviors, social interactions, communication practices, person-to-person exchanges

Not only does this mixture of tips help you engage different parts of yourself in your confidence efforts, it keeps things fun and interesting!

And how about this person giving you confidence advice? Why should you trust me? Well, I wasn't born with a confidence gene, that's for sure. I've fought, and tested, and pushed—and buckled at the knees at times working at my self-confidence. But today I'm living it because I practice *every day*. I'm inhabiting a confident place. And compared to that person—that old version of me—who used to sit on the sidelines and watch interesting things happen to other people, now I'm *doing things* that really interest me, that I dreamed of, and that light me up.

I want the same for you, however you might define it.

The advice here is more than anecdotal—it draws on coaching and training thousands of professionals on leadership and confidence at places like the World Bank, Under

Armour, HP, Microsoft, the US Treasury Department, and dozens and dozens of others. It comes from interviewing scores of executives for my previous books and conducting leadership research around the world.

The advice here draws on my personal journey as a professional too. I've navigated giant, medium, and little boutique employers—and along the way, I've been promoted, I've been laid off, I've supervised people, and I've had terrific bosses and horrible bosses. An important part of my lens is that I'm a woman of color. I've felt invisible and underestimated at work, and I've also felt the joy of carving out my own path to leading. All of that comes into play in *Quick Confidence*.

I'm an eat-cake-before-dinner kind of person. I want the diet Coke *and* the french fries. I believe in enjoyment (even if I think wine and coffee count toward my daily water intake).

I think we should put our authenticity and wholeness before any one job, manager, or career phase. I don't think there's any job that should require you to hang up who are on the coatrack—or that's worth trampling your well-being over.

I know that each of us can express something truly special and unique—that we can do big things by making regular deposits in our confidence. When we do, there's *no avoiding* those deposits becoming mighty sums of confidence that pay dividends for the rest of our lives.

One thing I like to tell myself when I'm heading into a big negotiation or high-stakes opportunity is, *Selena, walk in like you 400% belong.* It changes my posture, my stride, my facial expression—heck, even my contributions. It's how I make my presence felt.

*Now, it's time to make **your** presence felt.*

Walk with me into *Quick Confidence* like you 400% belong—because you do. Let's do this together. If you learned more about Greek archaeology than you did about self-worth in school, it's not too late for you. *Not at all!* Now is the perfect time to take your confidence journey bite by bite. Morsel by morsel even. Knowing that the best return on investment you'll ever get is the one you make in yourself.

1 Make Strong First Impressions

If you've ever sat there, sweating in a blazer, while people lob difficult questions at you, *you get it*. Those special things called job interviews are just one example of the first impressions that can feel "make-or-break" in your career. How is it that so much can ride on other peoples' 30- or 60-minute assessment of you as a human being? And how can a simple Q&A have such a disproportionate impact on your bank account, résumé, and future? We job candidates have our own power and agency (like the ability to walk away or not apply in the first place), but it's easy at moments like this to feel like *they have all the power*.

It's no wonder that situations like this make our heads spin with tension! In so many career moments, you *are* being sized up by others in a matter of minutes. But what makes this even trickier is that the rules are ambiguous: at a networking event, for example, we're told to present ourselves in an assured, confident way—but at the same time, we shouldn't come off as over-rehearsed or like a try-hard. And in pursuing a new role, just because we may want a job, we shouldn't convey that we *need* the job. Then, on our first day of a new job, we should make sure to dress in a smart, polished way, but we're cautioned about looking overly formal or out of touch. Talk about mixed messages!

The human need to search for acceptance from others, even early on in an interaction, is real. We evolved in such a way that sharing resources with other members of our group led to stronger social bonds and helped a group's chances of survival. Part of *today's* challenge comes from the fact that meeting new people means negotiating lots of unknowns. As NYU researchers explain it, each new person we meet is "a source of ambiguous and complex information."[1] It's sitting with that ambiguity, along with our compulsion to be accepted, that can push and pull our confidence levels like warm taffy. As we try to find that ideal, Goldilocks level of confidence in first-time interactions—not too much and not too little—we can end up forgetting to bring our actual, full, living, breathing selves with us. Not just in interviews, but in any meaningful first-time interaction—introducing ourselves to a prospect, meeting our new boss, or at a coffee date with someone who has the job we dream of having.

This happened to me right at a time when I was trying to cement an important consulting assignment and build up my business. I had done a small job for a midsized tech company—helping to launch a new employee resource group. I now had the chance to pitch a bigger, more powerful leadership and inclusion project to the CEO and his team. In that meeting with the CEO, I worked so hard on making my first impression memorable that I practically tried to fill that vast, gray conference room with my years of knowledge! Armed with my 64 slides, I was so caught up in a gust of "experting," I didn't leave many openings and spaces for his questions or comments. And slowly, I watched him kind of pull away from the conversation, literally backing his chair away from the table. As he did, my own negative self-talk went into overdrive—which caused me to give a particularly incoherent response to the single question he *was able* to ask! It hurts to admit, but as you probably can guess, I failed that day to both impress and make an impact.

Yes, it stung. But I can see more clearly now that any situation where you're driven by your insecurities and leading in someone else's style—not yours—will put you closer to losing your audience. Maybe you can relate? Have you ever played a false part initially—or watered yourself down to give others what you *thought* they wanted?

Part of the issue here is that we pressurize first impressions so much. After all—as undoubtedly you've heard—you never have a second chance to make a first impression, right? In the span of time it takes to bake brownies, we should somehow neatly downplay our flaws and peccadillos and showcase only our shiniest, most motivated, brilliant self.

Here's the thing. So many of the common narratives around making great first impressions are packed with covering up who you really are—and by extension, shaming the not-presentable parts. Well, I'm here to tell you that doesn't work. You do not need to pull one over on people to make it. And to think you should only hurts your confidence long term.

Drawing from my own lessons and from coaching and training thousands of leaders along the way, I'll illustrate how to show *all the way up* in these meaningful moments— get ready for it—*as yourself.* Whether you're trying to make a strong initial impression at a networking event—or on your first day at work, at college, or with a new client—you can do this best *as you.* And I can't wait to show you how.

Just Do You

So, let's update the mindset you're working with. Let's embrace a little thing called human, authentic first impressions. As we do, I hope you'll give yourself and others some latitude. Because who among us doesn't have "off" days and moments? Or doesn't stumble, stammer, or feel plain weird, sometimes, socially speaking?

While you're at it, make some room for the possibility that if things don't go just perfectly, the situation isn't chiseled permanently in marble. In fact, right now, cozy up to the idea that if you need to, you can deepen your existing impressions and relationships with people, even ask for a redo or strategize a comeback. And if for some reason you can't do those things, you know what? You'll learn that's survivable too.

 Adopt Dog Code

Sometimes the best confidence lessons come from the most unlikely places. Here's a case in point: Have you ever noticed how dogs greet us humans? If they're anything like my Newfoundland pup Midnight, they don't hesitate. They don't overthink it. They don't talk it over with their friends before making a move.

A dog's nature is to be the *first* to make a connection. To come right up to you and greet you. And I think there's an important confidence insight we can take from that.

After navigating a pandemic, we're all acutely aware of the importance of something scientists call "Vitamin S."[2] The need to bring people together socially, whether virtually or in person, and to feel a sense of togetherness.

In fact, scientists have discovered even *very subtle* interactions with strangers improved well-being![3] For example, in experimental studies where subjects were instructed to greet, smile, or initiate a very brief conversation—a *single* encounter—the interaction boosted people's happiness. These little moments included interacting with a bus driver, with fellow commuters on a bus or train, and with a barista at a coffee shop—even or being with a fellow participant waiting to take part in an experiment. Here's what's cool: the short-term boost in happiness occurs not only in the person initiating the conversation, but also in the person whose social contact was sought![4]

So how about it? Why not be the first to:

- Say hi and introduce yourself in a group?
- Invite your new colleague to a networking or learning session you're attending?
- Notice someone who's isolated and might appreciate an invitation to join you?
- Invite your new coworker to lunch?
- Be warm and welcoming to an employee your team's had a less-than-great relationship with in the past?

As you adopt "dog code," you may need to be courageous. Sometimes it feels vulnerable to be *the first*. If you're more introverted or reserved, it might feel challenging to "go right up" to perfect strangers and start speaking. *But you can still do it*. You might also need courage to challenge the culture of your organization or team—especially if being friendly or "being the first" is not the norm. It takes nerve to buck the status quo! But when you proactively welcome others, you show humility, curiosity, bravery, and a collaborative mindset. These are some of the best traits of true leaders.

Dog code won't just raise up your confidence levels, it's a way to override similarity bias too. Also called "mini-me syndrome," this cognitive bias explains our tendency to gravitate to people who look and think like us[5]—which of course narrows our world, our thinking, and our connections. When we adopt dog code, we get that much closer to halting bias and preferential treatment. To make this happen, we *all* must contribute to positive, welcoming environments and make inclusive first impressions a real thing.

Being the first is a great way to build confidence around other people. When you do, you make relationships a priority in your life—and the people around you will notice and remember.

 ## Connect, Then Lead

Have you ever felt a kind of nibbling pressure to demonstrate you were smart? You know, to show people that you *know things*? I know I've been there—and my bullish performance in front of the CEO is a fitting example. When the stakes feel high, we tend to want to prove our strength first and above all else.

But here's a newsflash: That's exactly the wrong tack to use when we want to make a strong first impression!

In a study by Dr. Amy Cuddy at Harvard University,[6] she found that employees prefer leaders to show warmth first and demonstrate competence second. To get a little more granular here, warmth is represented by things such as friendliness, kindness, and politeness; competence is shown through ability, intelligence, and skills. As Dr. Cuddy explains, once an individual gets a read on a target's warmth, the individual uses those judgments to decide how to behave toward the target.

I like to think about it like this: being friendly and warm is like a door that opens up more possibilities—it puts other people at ease and opens their ears to hear what you have to say next. On the flip side, low warmth is an inhibitor. Even if you're highly competent, your likeability and trustworthiness are what drive others' partnership, followership, and willingness to vouch for you. A Zenger Folkman study[7] that looked at 50,000 managers found that "if you're seen as low-warmth, you have something like a one-in-2000 chance to make the top quartile of effectiveness as a leader."

So how do we demonstrate this kind of warmth, in a clear and compelling way? Here are some sign posts!

Physical indicators of warmth:	Verbal indicators of warmth:
• Hold steady, engaged eye contact 60–70% of the time	• Ask follow-up questions as a way to show interest in the speaker's thoughts and feelings
• Nod to show you understand	
• Smile to signal you're welcoming and bringing positive energy	• Express empathy, as in "I imagine that's a lot to manage/cover/deal with. . ."
• Lean in, slightly, to show you're interested and engaged in an idea or to encourage the other person	• Make your early statements positive, rather than about your long flight or bad night's sleep
	• Give sincere compliments

I can still remember my mentor telling me when I was in business school that the best way to be interesting is to be *interested*. And the more I interact with people, the more that phrase resonates. Friendliness and warmth are a form of showing interest. We feel it, in an instinctual way, when someone behaves in a friendly, "I want to get to know you" way. So remember, next time you want to make a firm impression in someone's mind, prioritize your connection with them ahead of dazzling them with your brilliance. Once you establish warmth, the strength of your hard skills is a welcome gift, not a threat.

 ## Give a Great Intro

When someone starts a meeting with, "Let's do a round of intros," is your honest reaction ever to cringe? Even though you could talk about your work or industry for 30 minutes straight?

The funny thing is that even the most knowledgeable professional, with a respectable number of years under their belt, can feel anxious about nailing their intro. Why is this? Here are the three most common trip wires I see:

1. Pressure: Too often, we feel the crushing expectation that we should absolutely nail our intro—or showcase every single facet of our value. I'm here to tell you to relax a little bit. Stop trying to fit it all in. If you're meeting a new coworker, for example, it's perfectly okay to give them a broad intro but to leave a little bit of intrigue.

2. Improvising: Don't just wing it. When it comes to your intro, writing down two or three clear sentences about your role, until it's firmly etched in your mind,

can help you deliver it in a cleaner, more self-assured way. Stand-up comedians are allowed to commit their best lines to memory—why can't we?

3. Drudgery: If you hate giving your intro, it shows. But if you watch people who do this well, they willingly "take the baton" of power in the situation. They enjoy sharing. They don't behave as though their intro is a frivolous waste of time or an indulgence. So think about an enjoyable element of your work—for example, what gives you pride in your role—and start there. Casey Erin Clark, a talented speaker, coach, and friend, even recommends imparting a pleasant flavor to your name—and to imagine tasting it as you give your intro, so you're sure to enjoy it!

To find the right words, Paola Pascual of Talaera, an international firm focused on teaching business English, offers a great framework for making a clean intro: Adapted from[8].

The three simple elements are:

1. Name
2. Title
3. Translating your impact into simple, nontechnical language

The third step is the most important. It allows people to digest your message (especially if they're not in your role, company, or function) and to see you as more than just a jumble of #corporatespeak. When you get ready to share your impact in step 3, some of the verbal connectors you can use include: "But really, I. . .," "It's all about. . .," or ". . . Which is a fancy way of saying . . ."

This sounds like:

- I'm Trevor Miller. I'm director of operations, which is a fancy way of saying that I make sure that the company is run in the most efficient way possible.

- I'm Neil Singh. I'm a talent acquisition manager. I find, recruit, and hire great candidates. It's all about making sure the team keeps growing nicely.

- I'm a Dierdre Jones, I'm a social media manager and oversee content strategy for our three biggest retail clients. But really, I help companies tell compelling stories about their brands.

See how this adds simplicity *and* authenticity? I encourage you to practice with a partner, friend, family member—even your doggy. If all that fails, try it in the mirror! Next time someone claps and says, "Let's do a round of intros," take a nice breath before you give yours, smile sincerely, and enjoy sharing.

Meet People Where They Are

There's a classic social worker saying I learned on the first day of my master's program: "Meet people where they are." The idea is that to engage any person, we need to start by observing where they are now—and to align with that, without judgment. That's the opposite of telling them how and where to be—or to convey in some way they're too slow or uninteresting, not operating like we do, or not meeting our expectations.

Here's what's cool about this concept: our bodies confirm better than any other part of us whether we're willing to meet someone where they are. Make a great first impression with these three techniques:

- **Turn toward them, fully.** You've likely been there before, and so have I: You're speaking to someone and you're engaged in the conversation—but only part of their body is turned to you. They may be swiveling their eyes, head, and neck to look elsewhere, or maybe their torso is twisting in another direction, or maybe their feet are pointed elsewhere. I'll tell you what: It feels lousy to be the person getting sparse attention. When giving divided attention in this way, it tells others you're not engaged and may be looking for a quick exit from the conversation. To avoid these moments, make a point to have your body "squared" to the individual who's speaking. That means from your face—to your torso—to your toes—you're fully facing them.

- **If you're seated, rise to greet a person**. Let's say you're sitting in a restaurant waiting for your mentor to arrive. As they approach the table, you have a few choices. You could verbally greet 'em while seated or shake their hand as you remain seated and they hover above you. Here's a better approach: When you're meeting in person, and particularly if a new person walks into the room, stand up to greet them. When you do this, you're signaling respect and basic acknowledgment of them.

That also helps you engage them on an equal level—eye to eye. That's important because sometimes sitting can come off as being passive or meek.

- **Match people's speed.** If for example, you're talking and walking with someone in the direction of the buffet at a networking event, try to align your walking speed with theirs. (Many restaurant hosts and hostesses are taught to do this, guiding you to your table *at your speed* rather than leaving you in the dust!) When you do this, you're being observant of their style and aligning with where they are. This might seem like a minor attending skill but the impact is major. Similarly, if they're communicating in a way that reveals they're a slower talker, they probably won't appreciate a volley of 15 rapid-fire questions. Notice their pace and try, in little ways, to respect it.

When you meet people where they are, it's like you're saying, "I see you, *and* I respect you as you are." People may not know the principle you're using, but they'll know you care and you fully showed up.

 ## Start from the Inside Out

Your inner voice—your self-dialogue—is a funny thing. It can distort your weaknesses, amplifying your worst fears. Or it can support and encourage you, powering some of your biggest breakthroughs.

While most of us think of a first impression as something that manifests outwardly—it really starts with what we're saying inside. To help clients start to embed empowering beliefs in their minds, I have them repeat short sound bites, or mantras, over time. The great thing about mantras is that they really can become our new default programming like a new channel we're tuned into, mentally. And research suggests that affirmations can help you improve problem-solving under stress.[9]

So invest even a few minutes of time before your next "first impression" contemplating the new and improved qualities you're developing. You can practice reciting—and really internalizing these four messages:

1. **"I earned my place here."** When we feel we're on equal footing—just as entitled to be in the room and at the meeting table as others—we authorize ourselves to have a voice. Without this foundation though, we might undercut our words or backstep what we just said. So say with pride and even more emphasis if you need to, *"I totally earned my place here!"*

2. **"I take bold action in spite of fear."** Fear is not an omen that something terrible is sure to happen to you. It's normal and even something you can learn to shrug at. See your fear as a well-meaning but overprotective parent. And then challenge yourself to think and act big in spite of it.

3. **"If I take a wrong turn, I can right myself."** Sometimes it's not the challenge itself that's terrifying, it's the idea of recovering from failure. Well, here's a different way to look at it: Did you know cats have a "righting reflex" that allows them to orient themselves, no matter how thrown they are, so that they land on their feet? The same is true for you. If you're thrown off course, you have a ready set of skills, experiences, and instincts to help you rebalance.

4. **"If it's meant to be, it's up to me."** You are the number one agent of change in your career and life. Your own self-directed action is most potent. So don't wait for someone else. Claim that up-for-grabs power that's sitting on the table!

Remember, if your compassion doesn't include yourself, it's incomplete. Reprogramming your inner mind with empowering, motivating statements is one of the best gifts you can give yourself. It reminds of what you value about yourself and helps you focus on what you can control. And it helps you create the kind of supportive inner environment that unleashes your success. Not once in a while, but as your resting state.

 ## Be the Expert on Your Audience

Think of someone you've seen who made a great initial impression with a group they were convening or presenting to. They probably prepared mentally. The person probably knew their facts. But here's something extra-extra I bet they did: They spoke to the conversation the audience members were having in their own minds!

When you can peer into the minds of your audience before a networking session, presentation, or meeting, it shows. Your connection with the audience will strengthen. And you'll exude credibility and confidence.

So how do you deliver compelling and memorable messages by aligning with your audience's thinking? Try asking and answering these three questions ahead of time:

1. **The first question to ask yourself about your audience is: What are their main goals?** What are the

basics they're in charge of? This work is often at the forefront of their minds. Let's say you're presenting to the marketing department, a group that works on building awareness, engaging customers, and designing promotional activities—now, you can tailor bits of your conversation to acknowledge that. By dropping in these details, it strengthens your bond and trust with the audience.

2. **The second question to ask yourself about your audience is: What are they craving?** What is it they're particularly passionate about or hungry for right now? Sticking with our last example, let's say the marketing department is heavily fixated on competitor activity at the moment. By integrating terms related to competition into your conversations—such as "competitive advantage," "gaining an edge," or "beating out rivals"—it links you to the audience. They feel like you know the most pressing aspects of their world.

3. **The third question to ask yourself about your audience is: What are their pain points?** What obstacles are front and center for them? For most marketing departments, generating traffic and leads is a common, ongoing challenge. You might not have the cure to their problem, but even acknowledging their "pain" can boost your credibility in their eyes. You can highlight one of your own challenges, then relate it to one you know they have, like an ally would do.

If you don't know your audience's goals, cravings, and pain points—be creative. Interview a colleague who does know. Research corporate websites, press releases, even open job descriptions to understand what a particular group most needs at the moment.

When you empathize with someone else early on, you see the world more like they see it. You don't force your way on them. And that cements a positive first impression. In the words of computer scientist Alan Kay, "A change of perspective is worth 80 IQ points."

 ## Harness Halloween Confidence

People often comment on the brightly colored clothes I regularly wear. Now, it's not that I want to be seen from outer space—or take out your retinas. It's that bright colors make me feel energized, confident, emboldened, and engaged!

Just like me, your appearance tells a story. And that story doesn't just influence others: it influences how you see yourself. In one of my favorite studies,[10] conducted at Northwestern University, researchers found that students did better on tests that measured attention span and accuracy when they wore a white lab coat. The lab coat, which symbolizes care and attentiveness in the world of medicine and science, actually elevated the student's efforts. Wow! Subjects "embodied" the traits of the outfit they were wearing and were even more engaged and better at concentrating in tests.

Suddenly, I can appreciate why my Wonder Woman Halloween costume as an eight-year-old felt so awesome—and so real. My outfit didn't feel like "dress-up" or a costume; in it, I felt like the best version of me. Think about how you felt as a kid on Halloween: Did you have a favorite costume? How did it make you feel? Did it change how you walked, how you spoke (even as you asked for candy)?

Now, what can we learn from this? We already take on personas all the time—we already "play the part." The question is: how about proactively picking more positive personas with our clothing choices so that we feel our best and control *how we show up*?

So I want to know, what clothes make you feel most confident and engaged? For me, this means creating power outfits—ensembles that make me feel awesome! Here are two surefire steps for how you can build your own!

Step 1: Start by remembering a time when you wore something in a work setting and felt great. Maybe it's relaxed shirt in a calming tone, or a bold pattern that people always comment on. It's the fit or cut that feels "just right." Remember, what works for me will very well be different than what works for you. Alright, have you got it? Great.

Step 2: Now, I want you to try to identify and replicate that "feel-great" premise. Let's say what makes you feel best is a simple, well-cut, dark-colored trouser with a quietly patterned top. How could you create five or six iterations—combinations—of that look? If it sounds simple, it's because it is.

Whether your power outfits become your daily uniform or are reserved for big moments is up to you. I'm not going to tell you what's right or wrong. Instead, I'm going to say this: you get to decide. And what you decide to wear will affect how you feel. If you feel authentically *you* in your clothes, you'll bring that originality to work. Your confidence can come through in your conversations. Your presence and first impressions can change.

Experiment tomorrow with wearing those clothes and see if it changes how you feel.

Make Memorable Virtual First Impressions

Did you know people have 250% more meetings every day than they did before the pandemic?[11] Shocking, right? But just because we have more meetings, doesn't mean they're easier to negotiate.

That's especially true for virtual meetings.

When we lose some of our human signals in virtual settings, it can lead to more misunderstandings or ambiguity, and it can make us less sure of how and when to insert ourselves into the conversation. If you can relate to feeling this way, you're so not alone!

Here's the great news. You don't need to be a Zoom maestro, tech expert, or shapeshifter to handle virtual meetings and first impressions with aplomb.

Use these two go-tos the next time you want to start on the right foot in a virtual meeting:

1. Introduce yourself early:

According to the primacy effect,[12] humans have a tendency to remember better those things presented at the beginning of a sequence (compared to say, the middle). So, if you want to be remembered, think strategically about what you say early on. This can be as simply as saying, "Hi, it's Sharma Elliot, good to see everyone!"

Not just that, speaking up and introducing yourself or your contribution in the meeting quickly breaks a seal. It tells people (including you) that you're here, you have something to say, and you should be listened to. I find this "early gains" effect is amplified when I arrive a few minutes early and engage in small talk with folks as the meeting is getting going. It tells your brain, "I've already spoken so doing it more is NBD (no big deal)."

2. Shoot for at least three interjections:

Now, it's awesome that you piped up early with an intro. But there's one more thing you need to do. To make a strong virtual impression, you need to grab hold of the entire "impression time window" available to you. So challenge yourself to contribute three times. If you're a subject matter expert or otherwise have lots to say, no need to stop there. But to hit your goal of three, you can speak up by building off someone else's idea: "What I'm hearing from Carlos is X, and what's striking about that is. . .," synthesize different ideas: "I see points A and B as related, and that matters because. . .," or make a new connection: "This is sparking ABC idea, and I think we should take a look at it . . ."

These contributions can help you be seen and heard—even in spaces that are harder to navigate. Commit to these habits, and don't be afraid to take it one step further—share with at least one of your teammates your goal to show up in virtual spaces. Then encourage them to act as an accountability buddy.

 ## Be Ready for Opportunities

Most of us can think of someone who gets amazing opportunities—it's like no matter what they do or wherever they show up, good fortune just seems to fall in their lap.

How irritating, right? Especially if you feel like you're stuck in a spiral of bad luck.

Well, I'm willing to bet that the "luckiest" person in your life is a doer, not a hoper. Someone who's ready, even when making a first impression, to seize on a moment.

Think about it: juicy moments are everywhere—meeting someone from a cool company and inquiring if they're hiring, telling someone about your ambition, or asking to be part of a committee you just learned about. So how can you maximize these moments, rather than freeze up?

- **Be a giver.** In Dorie Clark's book *Stand Out*, she shares that lucky people are willing to approach others *without* expecting anything in return. Coming from a place of generosity with your network—rather than focusing on "what's in it for me?"—can create tons of goodwill, and, well, opportunities! Even in a first meeting, a willingness to send people valuable resources, to react compassionately to their circumstances, and to make needed introductions can go a long way. So give to your network as you make early impressions and watch as opportunities shine upon *you*.

- **Grab moments before the window closes**. There is a beautiful concept from ancient Greece called kairos (or καιρός)—it means "the right, critical, or opportune moment." In the space of one little breath, you can make a pivot or a move that changes everything. Lucky people are prone to grab those moments and find the opportunity in them—to act! Let's say you have one shot with an influential executive at your company. You're going to an event where they'll be, and you want to share your big new idea with them. This is the time to act (not overthink). So remember, an important piece of "luck" is a willingness to take bold action—to grab hold of the moment—in a timely way.

- **Change up your routines.** Over the longer term, this habit can create new experiences and widen your net of opportunities and connections. Check out a new coffee shop, take a different route to work, or go to a different networking event. These small changes can alter the people whose paths you cross and, by extension, your opportunities.

Have you ever changed your life and opportunities with one small decision? Have you ever made a bold first impression simply by being ready? Experiment with these tips to grab more of them.

2 Create Belonging Wherever You Go

Have you ever craved to fit in—even ached for it?

For as long as I can remember, I've been on a search for a sense of belonging—of fitting in. I'm half Pakistani on my dad's side. My mom is Caucasian and Ukrainian American. Put that all together with a sprinkle of Philadelphia thrown in, and you have me. (Don't worry, I have a healthy and equal respect for samosas, pierogies, and cheesesteaks.)

While there are plenty of cool things about growing up in a culturally blended home, one reality is that I never felt like a full, card-carrying member of either of my parent's communities. I wanted to belong in each one, but I just wasn't like the others.

Not just that, but growing up in a largely white community and school, I was hyper aware of the ways my household was different: our varied skin colors, the languages spoken at home, the smells of our food, and the lingering glances people gave my opposite-complected parents.

Just like many kids from multiracial homes will tell you: it's easy to feel like you don't fit in anywhere.

As a preteen, I can remember checking off the race/ethnicity section on state testing forms. None of the choices fit my "half and half" status, so I picked OTHER. I've done that many times since—and it always makes me feel like a Martian.

Another time, after arriving at college, I remember asking myself, "Should I join the South Asian student group?" only to find myself retorting, "Don't be ridiculous, you're only half."

Then, not very long ago, I was explaining an old, negative remark someone made to me as a kid about my brown skin, when the listener replied, "Wait, you're brown?!" Oof. That comment definitely triggered a mini identity crisis for me. Here, I thought it was obvious that I have beigey skin. Was I white-presenting, and hadn't even realized it? It was a potent reminder that the way people read you from the outside can have an impact on what you know about yourself. I have to admit, I felt more confused about my identity than ever!

Now, your desire to belong may be different than mine—but when it comes down to it, we all have experiences of feeling like we didn't fit in or weren't fully embraced or accepted. In every workshop I facilitate on inclusive leadership, I have people answer this prompt: "Think of a time you felt you didn't belong." And no matter how different the people are in the room, they can easily recall a time. For some, they came from a family of doctors but didn't want to carry on the legacy. For others, they never felt they fit in with their jock brothers and covered up the fact that they were naturally sensitive, not brash or aggressive. Some felt overtly left out because of their skin tone—or because they were gay—or "different." I'll never forget one man telling me how out of place he felt as a school kid because he was so poor, he didn't own (or wear) a pair of shoes.

Some of the kernels of wanting to belong are universal. The need to be accepted and seen—to be as worthy as the next person—and the need for people to hear, "You're one of us!" As I marched into adulthood, I continued my search for belonging. In my first roles as a management consultant, I advised executives in mahogany boardrooms on how to better engage their talent. There I was, young, brownish, five foot two—and I couldn't help but notice I looked the opposite in every way of the leaders I was advising.

That, plus my own youthful self-consciousness, made me certain I didn't belong. So I stopped offering my best ideas. I stopped making good guesses. I stopped wearing the bright clothes I love. I stopped being me.

Mentally, I had relegated myself to the "kids' table." I got very good at giving people the watered-down, diet Sprite version of me. Sitting in the outside rim of chairs. Mimicking other people's style. Downplaying my own. Everything about me was muted. Yawn!

Not only did I *feel* watered down, they weren't getting anything memorable from me either! They weren't getting my passions or strengths—my best ideas—or what makes me unique. As for me? I didn't have the satisfaction of bringing my best. I felt blah. Constricted and constrained. Tired of conforming.

What impact does *shrinking to fit in* actually have?

Sometimes you can shrink and pretzel—and origami yourself—so much that you're no longer seen or detected! Sure, you might be "presentable," but you have all the flavor of lukewarm water. Bor-ing! That makes it awfully hard to leave a powerful or lasting impression.

Slowly, something started to become clear in my mind—almost like a mental tattoo—after I'd been out sick for three days and no one noticed.

If your presence doesn't make an impact, then your absence won't make a difference.

Think about it, if your presence doesn't even register in the room, how can anyone know the real you? Or the value that you bring?

And along the way, I saw other groups struggling with the same dynamic I did. Marginalized folks who felt pressure to fit in. LGBTQIA folks. Immigrants. People of Color. And more. They learned to play themselves down in favor of emulating the most socially accepted.

It made me rub my hands together and think, "Wait a minute! *This* is a conversation I would like to facilitate. Between workers who want to bring their *full*, technicolor selves to work and leaders who want to create welcoming, inclusive environments where people can really contribute." That right there is the flashbulb moment that led me to quit my corporate job and start my own business, where I speak and facilitate workshops about leadership, inclusion, and belonging at companies and conferences.

Today it's a joy to get to facilitate more of those conversations—giving people the confidence to belong in any situation they want to be in—and to teach leaders how to create environments where people feel safe and respected. And me? I've finally learned how *good* it feels to bring my full, real self to my work. Yes!

If you've been holding back something that the world needs to know about—an idea, a dimension of you—it's time to embrace your power and confidence, to relinquish ambivalence. If you grew up in a home where you were taught to defer to authority, I know that this can be even harder. Right now, give yourself a little yellow piece of paper—a mental permission slip—that you can be confident in any situation, without anyone else's blessing. The only stamp of approval you need is your own.

Part of this is also deciding you'll use your confidence to show up for others. What I've learned is that we become even better at being inclusive when we make things personal, for example, when being an ally to those being harmed or excluded becomes part of our own code of conduct, set of morals, and leadership principles. Not some outer mandate. Or when we open up and tell someone about a time we screwed up an opportune moment of inclusion and what we've learned from it.

Yes, being more inclusive can be an overwhelming proposition at times. But that's exactly why I've cut these concepts into bite-size pieces and actionable tips in this chapter. These changes won't happen overnight, but small daily gains can make a huge impact—especially for people on the receiving end of biases or feeling sidelined in the margins. Whether you want to advocate more for yourself or someone else, don't wait for someone else to do it. You're more of an agent than you think. (Plus, no hero on a white horse is coming to the rescue!) Be the bold changemaker. It's time to start now. Let's start growing to stand out, rather than shrinking to fit in.

 ## Stoke Self-Belonging in Any Situation

Do you remember what it felt like when a thrilling career opportunity came your way? Maybe one so big you thought you weren't entitled to it?

Ten years ago, that was me. I was hard at work building my platform on leadership and inclusion, blogging each week, putting out a new book, and speaking to groups around the country. I can still remember sitting at my baby blue desk in my home office when I got a *thrilling* call!

It was a well-known tech company. They said, "Selena, we wonder if you'd like to interview to be our next global spokesperson."

Gasp! I was overjoyed. My heart rate zoomed into hyperdrive, and a flock of excited butterflies took off in my stomach. Just think about the impact this could help me make, opening up an important space to be more inviting and inclusive!

I prepped to go to New York City and meet and interview with the team. But as I got closer to the date, my self-doubts were *screaming*. And I couldn't shake them. I arrived for the interview, noticing I was the only person of color in this chic, slick restaurant. I remember thinking, "I'm not supposed to be here." And as the interview rolled forward, I psyched myself out of it. And it showed. I just wasn't selling what I was saying.

A few days later I got a polite email that said, "Selena, thanks for your time, stay in touch, but we're going in another direction." Ouch.

I realized (over lots of rosé and Oreos) that I misread my own blinking internal signal of apprehension and took it to mean I was unsettled, unqualified, and unfit.

There are two practices that helped me tame this dynamic (and thankfully prevent it from happening again). I recommend you take on these same actions to free your inner imposter from taking over:

1. **Name your critical inner voice and invite them forward to have a chat.** For me, my critical voice,

"Marjory," explained that she feels like she's protecting me from getting humiliated—which was surprisingly valid! Even so, I had to explain to her, "I get your concern—and thanks—but you're not helping like you think you are. I can, need to, and will override you."

2. **Adopt the following mantra in your day-to-day life, particularly when you doubt your enough-ness:** "I 400% belong here." I love this phrase. I say it with a fierceness, like I really mean it. I practically meditate on it before an important meeting or moment. For me, it's like soaking in a warm bath of acceptance, a reminder that "I'm a natural" in all kinds of environments.

As you cultivate your sense of self-belonging, regardless of the noise, events, or characters around you, you'll stoke a lasting kind of confidence. You'll start to quietly know you belong in any room you choose to enter.

 ## Be Conspicuous

Across the animal kingdom, there's a universal move to declare, "I'm powerful."

Now, I'm not referencing a signature bark, snarl, or squawk. I'm talking about *bigging up your body*.

Cats do this by standing upright and arching their backs. Wolves broadcast confidence with a stiff-legged gait and by holding their tail raised and outstretched. A bear blusters by carrying its head high, with its ears cocked forward, gaping its jaw open. When it comes to animals signaling strength, it turns out the body language of power is real.

And there's an important habit we can all borrow from our animal friends. The practice of engaging in expansive postures and gestures is so important, particularly when we're in a situation where others may communicate that *we don't belong*—or where we're doubtful ourselves that we should be there. It might feel intuitive or automatic to shrink down, but the last thing we want to do is constrict and narrow ourselves.

Quite the opposite, in fact!

One study[1] showed that adopting an upright seated posture in the face of stress helped subjects maintain self-esteem, reduce negative mood, and increase positive mood compared to a slumped posture. Sitting or standing upright is just one way to start an interaction on a confident note, but I'd suggest it can also help you be more resilient when you're feeling lousy, left out, or out of place.

For example, when you stand tall with your head elevated and squared up to your counterpart, you are signaling, "I'm not shrinking from this moment or situation. I'm here. I'm claiming my place." It's similar when we lean forward to make a point or express interest—or when we stand with our arms outstretched.

These habits make you feel more positive and present in the moment and they have an added benefit: they convey confidence and authority to those around you! Following are some of my favorite techniques for being conspicuous, easy to see, and for celebrating what your momma gave ya:

Constrictive behaviors	Expansive behaviors
• Seated perched on the edge of your chair	• Fully enveloping your seat with your back against the back cushion and arms on armrest

Constrictive behaviors	Expansive behaviors
• Sitting with hands crossed on lap or tucked underneath thighs	• Leaning slightly forward with palms exposed on table
• Protecting torso with crossed arms	• Open torso, shifts to face others
• Stooped/drooping posture	• Standing or sitting tall
• Bouncing or cautious eye contact	• Engaged and steady eye contact
• "Low talking"	• Easily audible, clear voice (7 out of 10 in volume)

By making some body language swaps like these, you send a meaningful signal to your brain that you are more than adequate or suitable. You're powerful! Make sure nobody—including yourself—forgets it!

 ## Engage in Power-Sharing

Not long ago there was an online viral trend with this prompt: "What's a deep quote from an unlikely source?" My answer? "Authority should derive from the consent of the governed, not from threat of force!" —Barbie, *Toy Story 3*.

So many workers today want more control—more consent, to use Barbie's term—over the way work gets accomplished. Over the way they're governed. And why shouldn't they, right?

Writer Annie Dillard famously said, "How we spend our days is, of course, how we spend our lives." Given that we spend a third of our lives at work, shouldn't those hours feel cooperative—shouldn't they be the product of a series of everyday collaborations, of mutual deals? Where power is shared?

The good news is that you can be the kind of person, no matter your level, who becomes known for power-sharing (even if those around you engage in power-hoarding!) Phew!

This requires bringing a more consultative approach with other people—which makes people feel part of things and like they matter. And it's a crucial component of helping them belong. So how does power-sharing look in action? How does it sound? The following quick reference explains some of the core differences in terms of behavior—with simple phrases that illustrate each behavior.

Power-hoarding actions and phrases	Power-sharing actions and phrases
Withholding context or the catalyst for an action "Going forward, we want you to change X."	Explaining "why" "Here's what motivated the change we're making . . ."
Making unilateral decisions "We've added the following step to our process."	Seeking people's input when decisions affect them "Based on your feedback, we're implementing this new step in the following way . . ."

Power-hoarding actions and phrases	Power-sharing actions and phrases
Reserving power for those at the top, such as leaving names off invitations and omitting people from distribution lists or notices	Pushing power, information, and responsibility downward
"I don't think we need to involve Margo at this time. Let keep things on a need-to-know basis."	"Margo, I know you have the most expertise on this topic. Can you join our meeting next week?"
Information is obscure or hard to get, based on norms of secrecy and territorial behaviors	People are transparent with information, and it's accessible
"This is my turf (and therefore this report is my info). Plus, sharing the report with others will just open a can of worms."	"Today we're sharing the data highlights with you from the report. But for those who want to dig deeper into the details, the report's stored on the shared drive. Let us know if you have questions."

When people model open, accessible actions as an everyday norm, it takes away some of the cliquey toxicity that damages even the most motivated person's morale. It gives people the clarity to do their jobs, the confidence to know they can raise an issue—the sense that *they belong*.

 ## Embrace the Compliment

Everyone knows that the risk of failure can be scary. What about the risk of *succeeding or being great*? Sometimes flying high can be just as scary as crashing. And sometimes that fear makes it so that *we exclude ourselves* from belonging!

Can you relate?

Maybe you've burnished a certain skill or experienced a win, and for whatever reason you were a little afraid to accept it. To absorb it. To own it.

That happened to me not long ago. Someone said, "I read your book in my leadership course at Cornell—it was great." Wow! "How cool," I thought, "I didn't even know it was being taught there!" Then something weird happened.

I found myself deflecting the compliment. Shrinking away a little from her words. Feeling like maybe it was a mix-up. I said, "Uh . . . my book? It came out in 2012. Are you sure you're thinking of the right one?"

Have you ever done that?

It probably won't surprise you that in one study in the *Journal of Experimental Social Psychology*,[2] people with low self-esteem had the most trouble warming to compliments. Why? Their own flawed, "not good enough" self-image didn't match up with the more positive image others had of them.

Well, I'm here to tell you that blocking compliments like you're a nonstick cookie sheet won't build your confidence or your self-esteem! And it won't help you feel you belong. It's not *just okay* to take a passive compliment, it's important to actively say yes to it. To embrace it—physically and mentally. Here are some simple ways you can better accept—and own—the praise you receive.

When you're getting some praise—turn toward it. Square up to the person giving it and allow yourself to be fully open to it, and to absorb it. Next, use the rule *"Thank you, and."* Rather than diluting (or devaluing!) the compliment you receive, say, *"Thank you,"* and then add one honest take of your own. That way, you let people "in" so they can see your authentic reaction. For example, if a newer person says upon meeting you, "I've heard great things about your work!" you could consider these do's and don'ts:

DON'T SAY:	SAY:
X "Oh it was no big deal."	✓ "Thank you for sharing that. I loved my time working on ABC project."
X "Anyone would have stepped up and done the same."	✓ "Thank you for the nice words. It means a lot to me."
X "Oh I was just doing my little part."	✓ "Thanks. I'm thrilled people are happy with X—I'm happy with how it turned out too."

See how the "do's" validate the compliment received *and* the compliment giver? If you're reflexively deflecting the praise you receive, you are cutting off a critical channel of information about your contributions, unique value, reputation, and performance! You're also effectively shutting down someone who has gone out of their way to appreciate you. So instead, see compliments as a data set of your strengths. Allow them to filter through your exterior and take up space inside. Then, use them to go further and start to proactively translate those strengths in new ways. And if you need an extra boost, invite your body to be conspicuous!

Assume Power Dynamics Are Always Present

Will you do a little thought experiment with me?

I want you to consider three teams. One team is known for promoting favoritism. Another team is known for fiercely hoarding information. A third team has a reputation for being fair-minded, with free-flowing conversation.

Which one has power dynamics present?

Here's an eye opener! They *all* do. Yep!

It's a common misconception to think that power dynamics only exist in dysfunctional workplaces. In fact, when I raise the topic of power dynamics, many clients will tell me, "Things are equal around here" or "Here? But nobody has egos . . ." or "We're not about power here." But think about it: even if you're the best manager on earth, you still decide who to hire and fire, who to promote, how to spend a budget, and what good performance looks like. And the people around you? They can't escape that fact, that power differential, no matter how awesome you are.

That's why as a leader and ally, it is so important—I mean vital—to adopt the mindset *that power dynamics are always present*. If you think about it, people who run really excellent meetings do this well. They assume that even if a group is behaving collaboratively, there are power dynamics. That even if a bunch of peers are meeting with no overt hierarchical differences, there are other power dynamics.

And they design meetings and meaningful moments with equalizing power dynamics in mind. So how does this look in action? It requires you to:

- **Become aware of your power and position.** Before you enter a situation, ask yourself, what power do I bring to this person or group—whether from my title, level of oversight, influence, or something else? How might that influence how others engage with me?

- **Divvy up airtime.** In a presentation or agenda, you can make sure *multiple* voices and perspectives are heard. Try slicing up speaking roles throughout the meeting or you could have different individuals own and run a meeting or series as the leader. Make sure to pay attention to some of the social or structural power dynamics in the meeting: are women and nonbinary people speaking as often as men? Are People of Color speaking as often as white folks?

- **Manage the over-talkers**. When you see an over-talker dominating the conversation, correct it and put the spotlight back on those who should have the floor. If overtalking is rampant, think about developing meeting norms that define positive team member behaviors so everyone can hold people accountable.

- **Create spaces.** Design meetings so there are dedicated openings for people to contribute throughout—you can ask, "What are your concerns? What are the opportunities you see?" Or you can always end with a catchall question: "What else? What did we miss today?" This is a great opportunity to call forward anyone who's been quiet so far. You could say, "Tanisha, I'd love to get your input. Do you have any thoughts on XYZ?"

- **Foster healthy disagreement.** Invite people to disagree with you by asking them to bring a contrary approach. This invitation gives them a license to shoot down ideas or challenge *the way it is*.

If you want to be known for truly great meetings and interactions, always assume power needs rebalancing. Then design with that in mind. Even if you're wrong, you will model and elevate what it means to be inclusive.

 ## Advocate for Overlooked Coworkers

The stolen spotlight. We've all seen it. Just recently I met with a team where a junior member had an exciting new idea she wanted to share. She mustered the courage to say it, but right when she got to the punchline, a more senior male talked over her. Her point got derailed, the moment was gone, and people forget what she was even talking about. Ouch.

Here's the thing: being an advocate for overlooked coworkers is a powerful way to shift the momentum—to make sure everyone feels welcome, included, and valued.

A person may be overlooked at work for many reasons. Perhaps they're new to the company and feel a little shy or they are naturally introverted and have a hard time speaking up in meetings. Maybe they're part of a marginalized group, and your other coworkers have too much unconscious bias in their morning coffee—every morning.

Here are three ways you can advocate for your over-looked coworkers and "spread the spotlight," drawing on the insightful work of Dr. Joan Williams, Distinguished Professor of Law at UC Hastings:

1. Give 'em a Strong Introduction

Make an effort to understand your overlooked coworker's professional history so you can highlight the main points when introducing them to someone new. You can remove a ton of pressure from your coworker's shoulders by starting the conversation *with them*. Not only does this ensure you mention what makes them great, but it gives them a few extra seconds to collect their thoughts before speaking.

Here's an example: "Janine has five years of event planning experience, and I'm excited to have her on this project!"

2. Shield Them from Critics

Sometimes, people think they have all the information or ideas they need, so they shut others out and make a decision with what they have. They don't realize the next idea might be the best one they've heard yet! Speak up if you know your overlooked coworker has proved their value in a similar situation, or they have the skills necessary to succeed in a new endeavor.

Here's an example: "Let's hear this idea out. I know Sam has run several full-cycle projects *just like this*."

If you aren't aware of their past successes, you can check in with them before, during, and after a meeting.

3. Nominate Them for Great Assignments

Don't wait for assignments to get handed out if you know who would be perfect for the job! Help connect people to assignments that will communicate their value where you can also be confident that the project is in the right hands.

Here's an example: "Erin managed a similar portfolio last spring, and she'd be great at running point with the client."

See how these simple interventions move the
spotlight?

Remember, being overlooked hurts feelings, stalls
progress, and contributes to a toxic workplace. To give
everyone a truly equal opportunity means starting with
your own actions. To make a difference right now,
today—raise the overlooked up, so they're noticed when
it matters most.

 ## Develop Cultural Humility

Have you ever been corrected about something you said
and instantly felt regret?

It's a definite "facepalm" moment. Maybe you weren't
thinking clearly and made a gaff. Maybe you were moving
too quickly and forgot something important. It's kind of
mortifying, right?

That happened to me a few years ago, and it was an
unforgettable learning moment. I was working on a global
team when a teammate from Europe mentioned they
couldn't understand some of my phrases. I was weaving in
terms I thought were clear, such as:

- "FOMO" (fear of missing out),
- "Talking shop" (talking business), and
- "What a home run" (a hit in baseball that enables the
  batter to complete a circuit of bases and score a run. In
  other words, an impressive success).

What was natural shorthand to me didn't resonate in
other cultures. Why does this matter? Author Terence

Brake, says it best: "Communication only happens when meanings are shared."

As a leader and inclusion ally, your messages are only as good as they are understandable. How can you confidently shift your thinking to be more broad-minded in cross-cultural settings, so your messages reflect that too? Consider the following tips to stretch your mindset for different people and approaches:

1. **Be sensitive to your own leaps and assumptions.** Sometimes without even realizing it, we carry around an assumption that other people should operate, well, like we do! Or we may believe there's only one "right way." Rarely is this absolute thinking helpful in cross-cultural settings. Instead, when you are working with a new culture, start from a position of trust. When you trust, you assume positive intent—and you can build on that with curiosity. And those genuine, curious questions spark learning and break down barriers. This is a great way to halt your own assumptions about others!

2. **Avoid expressing yourself in slang.** Practice using universal terms in team settings for the benefit of all. Think about it: you can either create a glossary of terms everyone has to use or you can encourage people to use universal terms in team settings (which one sounds easier?). So instead of talking about how you'll build a "strawman of a plan," say you're creating an outline. Instead of saying you'd like to "address the first swim lane of the strategy," say you want to address the first section. If you see someone use a term that's hard to understand, pause and ask them to explain it for everyone's good.

3. **Reduce the feeling of distance.** You can invite far-flung colleagues in and reduce remoteness in several ways.

First, take responsibility for building the relationship.
Be the first person to welcome them and take time to
get to know them or learn about their culture. Second,
dedicate time to non-work dialogue. You can compen-
sate for the fact that you're not bumping into each other
by having a once-a-week virtual coffee/tea meetup.

As we become a more culturally complex world, it's up
to all of us to engage in self-reflection, learn about ourselves
and others, and purposely interact with diverse groups.
I love personal growth author Ken Keyes's take on it:
"Everything and everyone around you is your teacher."

 ## Perform Acts of Noncompliance

When the COVID-19 pandemic started, one of the ways I
pivoted my business was to do livestreamed weekly events
with thought leaders I respected. In my own life, I was feeling isolated and cut off from people while in quarantine,
and doing live shows felt like a way to bring my community
together—and grow it—virtually.

The series got off to a running start, complete with
a show sponsor. Together with my team, I was learning
immensely about leadership from the riveting experts join-
ing me. Then I did a show with a guest who blew the lid off
my series, Madison Butler.

Madison, a sought-after equity strategist, explained how
earlier in her career, she interviewed with a company as a
recruiter. They were really enthusiastic afterward and called
her and said, "Oh my God, we love you, we really wanna
hire you, but . . ."

"But? But, but what?" Madison asked.

They said, "We need you to change your hair color, cover your tattoos, take out your nose ring, make sure your hair is straight, and wear a skirt." Uhh, holy prejudice, Batman!

To which Madison said, "That is a very long list."

The fact is, there are moments where people might tell you that you don't belong as you are. And in those hurtful circumstances—you have a few choices:

- You can dilute your essence and tone down what stands out.
- Or you can embrace the ever-living hell out of it.

The second option is exactly what Madison did.

After her interview experience, Madison, bedecked with gorgeous aqua-colored hair, asked herself, "Okay, how can I market myself so that people know that I'm not willing to change anything about my identity or what I look like? I'm really good at what I do, but I'm also really good at what I do *and* able to have blue hair at the same time." She decided to put "blue-haired recruiter" on her LinkedIn profile and when she started going to networking events, people began recognizing her—they said, "Oh my God, you're the blue-haired recruiter!" Today Madison is even more prolific, successful, and well known by her evolved moniker *The Blue Haired Unicorn*.

How about you? In the face of a situation where you might not fit, I encourage you to defy the "haters" and do more of . . . you. If someone says your self-presentation is lacking but you love it, be dogged that you'll honor what *you* want. Vania Phitidis, a coach and counselor, advises that doing this reminds your brain that you're living life on your terms. How? By performing acts of noncompliance with the predominant cultural rules of beauty or attractiveness.

She urges, "Cut or style your hair the way you've always wanted to, but haven't because you're afraid it'll emphasize your roundness. Wear something you've always avoided because the culture has led you to believe you can't get away with it. Choose a lipstick that you love, but haven't worn because society tells you to 'act your age.'" Basically, give standards the finger, and do you.

 ## Call People In and Call People Out

Imagine someone in your department makes an offensive, out-of-bounds remark at a team meeting.

Shudder.

What would you be most likely to do? Would you address it then and there with the group? Or pull the person aside and discuss it one-to-one? Would you maybe speak to their manager? Or would you be tempted to slowly scoot your rolling chair out of the room and flee?

Situations like this, especially when they go unaddressed, can crush a sense of belonging and morale. Yes, lots of people believe in right and wrong, but how many people truly step in and immediately *right* a *wrong*?

Well, I'm here to tell you, you *can do* something. Now if I just made your blood pressure go up a little bit, let me say this: confronting an issue where someone's being excluded or harmed does not mean you need to be perfect or flawless. In fact, I think all of us are braver when we take the stifling pressure off ourselves to be perfect!

So I want you to lean on a clear and powerful framework for dealing with exactly this type of situation. Developed by Dr. Loretta Ross of Smith College, this is referred to as *Calling in versus Calling out.*

Calling in is a way to explore deeper meaning with a person—to find a mutual sense of understanding or learn more. That could be used if, say, someone says something you don't fully understand, but it sits badly with you for some reason. Whereas *calling out* is a short and clear way of expressing concern or disapproval in the moment—for example, if someone just made a clearly prejudiced joke and you want to stop it right away. The following examples give you a sense of how each strategy sounds in action:

Calling in	Calling out
• "I'm curious. What was your intention when you said. . .?"	• "Hey, that's not cool. Please rethink what you just said."
• "It sounded like you said _____. Is that what you really meant?"	• "Please stop there. That's not how we speak to each other here."
• "How might other people interpret your words/actions?"	• "Wow/Nope/Ouch. I need to stop you right there."
• "Can we pause here and discuss your last comment?"	• "Those are not our values. That is not our culture here."
• "I don't find that funny. Tell me why that's funny to you."	• "Awwwwkward. I need to ask you to leave the room if you don't stop."

Look, Oscar-winning actors are allowed to memorize their lines, and you are too. Even if you only commit one or two of these to memory, you'll have a phrase on the tip on your tongue to confront exclusionary or harmful behavior. It's time for each us to step up without hoping someone else will do it. If not now, then when?

3 Rebalance Power Dynamics

"Excuuuuse meeeee!" an executive bellowed loudly, while pointing at his mug.

We were standing in a large, noisy conference room with at least a dozen other people swarming around before a big meeting. I continued laying out my notes since I was getting ready to present momentarily.

"Helloooo?" he looked directly at me. "A little help? This milk . . . is off."

Gah! With an uncomfortable smile, I said, "I'll let the receptionist know." Almost immediately, he smacked his head, sheepish, and said, "Oh, I thought you *were the receptionist.*"

Yeah, buddy, I could tell. But nope! In fact, that day I was presenting the findings of a global study I lead-authored for one of the largest companies in the world!

By his quick calculations, my power didn't match his. And it's not just me. For plenty of historically marginalized or underestimated people, they've been on the receiving end of people "rounding down" in terms of their stature, position, or degree, where people are making a mental shortcut that you are permitted less or carry a smaller designation.

This is only one example of the many moments when we can rebalance the power in the room, to change the way the scales are tipping, to correct a flawed perception, to reassert our role or place.

Of course, we all tend to be more cognizant of harm or damage that's overt: like people yelling slurs at someone in the street, someone being openly anti-Muslim as a blanket rule, threats or acts of violence against someone for their LGBTQIA status, or an individual who rejects a disabled person's resume outright based on their disability.

But so often, we're negotiating microaggressions that are quieter, smaller, that are much more subtle and indirect. At times they can even be unintentional. And they can be really hard to prove!

Here are some examples of microaggressions people have shared with me:

- A Hispanic male engineer meets his client for the first time and is asked by the client: "Are you sure you're the lead on this project? You don't look like an engineer."

- An openly LGBT interviewer interviewed a job candidate but the candidate wouldn't make eye contact and behaved dismissively. Despite the LGBT interviewer sharing the dismissive experience with his team, the other interviewers on the team had a positive interview experience with the candidate and suggest the candidate is advanced.

- A black woman takes issue with her sales territory being reduced and expresses frustration to her manager. She is told to "calm down" and asked why "she's so animated and angry."

There's no employee manual that tells you quite what to do in these situations. They are ambiguous, tricky, and uncomfortable. Not just that, but if you experience these slights often, the damage can have a cumulative effect. Think about it, a pattern like this can seriously affect the trajectory of a person's career. If you are constantly questioned, undervalued, and patronized by your peers, people are less likely to consider you for a promotion or exciting stretch assignment—no matter how much it's deserved. It can create, as Dr. Joan Williams of UC Hastings calls it, a slow escalator down in a person's career. (On the other hand, constantly being seen as high-potential and "leadership material," or people presuming your intelligence and skills, can create an escalator *up* in your career.)

On a personal level, when you're overlooked, spoken over, and diminished at work, it can prickle. You've worked just as hard as others—possibly harder—to get where you are. You deserve the recognition. Add to this the internalization of being underestimated—where for some people, they absorb the message that they are "less than." In a case like this, a person's assumed inferiority might make them opt out of high-level opportunities for fear they're not up for the job. Freaking awful, right?

No matter what industry you work in, it never feels good when someone assumes you're less qualified, experienced, or in a junior position, especially when it happens more than once. Yes, you might want to shout a few warranted expletives, but I promise there are ways to keep your interventions productive and to deliver them with confidence.

In this section, I'll offer you quick confidence tips that help you stay mindful—even if you're diminished. They're going to help you boost your attention and presence. They'll also help you maneuver more adeptly and remain open to the other person—each of these elements allows you to negotiate the best outcome in these challenging experiences—even if you have a power-monger sitting across from you!

So as you go, and learn to cope with even the most belittling bullies, bring these tools with you:

Your attention! When our minds are fully attending and focused (ahem, *not* multitasking on our phone while also trying to listen), we watch and consider what's happening right in front of us in a more complete way.

I'm also asking you to bring your *intention*. This is about looking inside, and knowing in a given situation what our aims and plans are. Not just flowing with the current of a meeting, for example, but having a sense before you walk in about what "hat" you'd like to wear, what way you'd like to operate with the group, or what you intend to convey or do.

And *presence*? That's one more thing I definitely want you to bring. It's about being in the moment, here and now. That means we don't mentally have 32 tabs open in our brain. If we're meeting one-on-one with someone, we're totally there, in that room, with that person.

And we all need a nudge at times to *stay open*, especially in situations where our knee-jerk reaction is to feel defensive. This means being curious and not reflexively making an evaluation right away, but starting with observing and noticing.

Bring these tools with you, and you'll find it much more natural to stand up for what you need. You won't just shift the balance of power more often in the rooms you enter; you'll find a deep and reliable reservoir of power in yourself.

Say Nope to Being Underestimated

If you're being underestimated again and again while you watch others climb and advance, it's time to put your foot down—*right now*. If someone assumes you're less than you are—in status or title—it requires taking action. This doesn't have to be complicated or require magical influencing powers either. If anything, standing up and shifting the power is something you can do with small actions. Here are my *top six* strategies for staying strong and resilient in these situations:

1. Use Reflective Listening

Let's say someone mistakes you for junior staff. Start by reiterating their statement back to them. For example, if someone relegates you to an administrative task, you can say, "So you're asking that I order the lunch?" You can then explain how seeing you're the highest-ranking manager (or fill in the blank), it's not the best use of your time. It'll open a conversation for you to make them aware of their mistake.

2. Focus on the Task at Hand

You have a job to do at the end of the day, and your colleague's attitudes are hindering your performance. You can make them aware of this by saying, "I'm really trying to get X done, and I'm not feeling very motivated when you constantly assume I'm underqualified."

3. Get Some One-on-One Time

Getting a coffee or lunch with someone who makes incorrect assumptions about you is probably the last thing you want to do, but it can make a huge difference. Even just one conversation can give this person a chance to know you on a deeper level—and will make them likelier to consider your perspective.

4. Be Direct

Sometimes the best way to correct someone is to just get it out. Be polite but firm. "I have worked hard to be in X position, and I won't have you undercutting my success. Please do not refer to me as X again." *Mic drop.*

5. Work on a Project Together

When you're given the lead on a project, try to engage with the person who mistakes your position on your team. This will allow you to show your skills in action, so they won't make that mistake again.

6. Go to the Boss or HR (But Remember HR Is Not Your Friend)

If you are continuing to experience disrespect and microaggressions from a colleague or coworker, you might have to approach the big dogs—with caution. Make your boss or HR aware of the situation along with documented evidence of how this person is treating you. As you build a case, remember HR has their own interests protecting the company—don't see them as a savior!

Constantly fighting injustices at work—for instance, simply wanting to be seen for who you are—is exhausting. But we have to continue standing up for ourselves and other people and groups who are made to feel small. Just remember, you worked incredibly hard to be here. You earned your way into your role. No snide comment or incorrect assumption can take that away.

 ## Hang up the Apology Habit

On a recent morning, standing in line at a coffee shop, I barely brushed the barista's wrist as I handed him $10. "I'm sorry!" immediately came out of my mouth. My nine-year-old daughter looked up at me with a no-nonsense look and said, "Momma, what do you have to be sorry about?!"

Whew, did she call me out. From the mouth of babes, right?

Do you ever automatically find yourself saying "I'm sorry"—if you can't make it to a meeting, if you can't accommodate a last-minute request, even if you're taking a "little too long" to decide on your order at a restaurant?

One problem with over-apologizing is that it can lessen others' respect for you. Of course, a heartfelt apology is meaningful and necessary at times, but a constant stream of saying sorry is not.

The other issue is that overdoing it with apologies can be self-reinforcing. When we say it enough, it can become a little too believable that, in fact, we are in other people's way, that we're a bother or that we shouldn't be taking up their time—that *they have all the power.*

In honor of stopping the apologizing madness in my own life, here are five verbal swaps I've made that have profoundly freed me and upped my power. I hope you'll join me in adopting them!

Instead of:	**"I just wanted to share . . ."**
Try:	"I want to share . . ."
The logic:	So often, we say "just" to soften up a direct, assertive message. The problem is, it demeans whatever we have to say with it.
Instead of:	**"I may be wrong, but . . ."**
Try:	"Here's what I know today . . ."
The logic:	We could all be wrong, at any time, about anything. That doesn't mean we need to lead with it—it's better to focus on what you do know.
Instead of:	**"Sorry to bother you . . ."**
Try:	"When you have a moment, I'd like X."
The logic:	You're not a bother for interacting with colleagues—collaboration is how we accomplish countless things today. Even if you are bothering someone, trust they'll let you know a better time or when they can get to your request.
Instead of:	**"Does that make sense?"**
Try:	"What are your thoughts/reactions?"
The logic:	Rest assured, you do make sense. If people have a question, they'll let you know. What you can't know are others' thoughts and reactions, so ask about that.
Instead of:	**"I hope that's OK . . ."**
Try:	"Thanks for considering it."
The logic:	You can be consultative without asking other people for permission. Instead of transferring approval to them, ask them to consider your request and thank them.

The less I over-apologize, the better I feel. It's liberating to shake off the feeling you're constantly stepping on someone's toes. Or that your need for information is inconveniencing people. #SorryNotSorry!

 ## Rock a Resting Neutral Face

To watch professional poker player Vanessa Rousseau compete in a live event is a pretty awesome thing. Not only is she a master strategist with each precise move (and a notable track record of wins), but her look is compelling: while playing the game she wears headphones, a hat, and dark sunglasses, all while maintaining a completely expressionless face!

See, just like Vanessa, each of us has *tells*, little micro-behaviors that tell others what we're thinking, feeling, or what we plan to do next. And while Vanessa might go far out of her way to conceal her tells (and it probably isn't practical or appealing for you to wear sunglasses at work), there's something all of us can learn from her practice.

Lots of the professionals I train tell me that when they feel diminished or receive a disappointing or unsatisfactory answer, they feel some pressure in that moment to still be congenial, to be a team player. That might mean showing up as agreeable, accommodating, or acquiescing.

The trouble is, if we've just been slighted, for example, we got a "No" to our fair and well-deserved raise request, it drains our power to force ourselves to act sweet and agreeable!

If you're someone who feels pressure to be warm, smiley, and friendly—even if you're hearing something you don't like, I want to encourage you to try out what I call a resting neutral face, or RNF.

Like a poker face—an RNF means your face is neutral. Your brows are relaxed, your lips are closed but not clenched—and in this case, your eyes are making steady, engaged eye contact. You are not frowning—but you're not smiley either.

When you do this, you level the power in the room. You show you're impartial (until you reach a conclusion), that you're deliberating about what you heard. If, for example, your manager just told you you're getting the worst pay raise in the history of pay raises, showing them an RNF while you think through your response can be really effective. You're not conveying support for their news, but instead you're creating some suspense—where your manager doesn't know how you're feeling. And that works to your advantage.

Plus, I promise, you don't look as excruciatingly weird as you think you do. When you're engaging in a moment of silence, with a neutral face—you look considered, thoughtful, as if you're reflecting. And that is not a bad thing. If this is tricky for you, try to consciously relax your feet—then move up to your calves and then upper legs, to give your mind something to do while you relax and neutralize the expression on your neutral face.

This is better than nodding or smiling in the moment—which might betray how you're really feeling—pissed off, disappointed, and undervalued. Resisting the urge to reassure people with your expressions (even if they just screwed you over) takes practice though. In my workshops, I have learners experiment live with using an RNF. And it's not uncommon for it to start out awkward and uncomfortable and end up being deeply liberating and empowering.

Remember, sometimes the bigger power move is to do *less*.

The next time you disagree with how things are going, don't feel pressure to nod, be agreeable or look overly cooperative. Through your eyes, face, and body, reinforce that you have choices. Teach people how to treat you. Teach people you have power because you *do*. Bam.

 ## Manage Invasive Questions

"Why haven't you gotten married yet?" *Excuse me!?*

"When are you having kids?" *How is that any of your business!?*

"Why have you been going to so many doctor appointments lately?" *Uh, WHAT!?*

Invasive questions at work are awkward. Sure, they can sometimes come from a kind, interested place. But understandably, most people want to be able to assert their boundaries and choose what's up for discussion and what's not.

Whether it's an interaction with a new person or someone you know well, I would like to make something abundantly clear: *You* are allowed to decide what people can ask you about. You carry lots of power here! You don't have to answer any question you don't want to, and you don't have to give a reason why.

If you're put on the spot and a question feels highly personal or out of bounds, remember you can be civil while dodging it. Your well-being, self-respect, and boundaries matter too much!

Try out these comebacks:

1. **Answer the question with a question:**

    "What makes you ask?"

    This tactic gives you control over the way the conversation goes. Now, the asker has to explain why they're so interested in your personal life. Plenty of times they'll self-reflect and step off.

2. **Make them aware of how inappropriate their question is:**

    "I'm surprised you're comfortable asking someone that."

    Laugh it off to show you don't want any tension. Or offer this statement and walk away.

3. **Be direct:**

    "I don't feel comfortable answering/talking about that."

    Short and sweet. Tell 'em like it is. You don't have to explain yourself further, and they most likely won't press your button again once they know your limits.

4. **Give them a taste of their own medicine:**

    If someone asks you why you must go to the doctor again, ask them what their last doctor appointment was for. Some people might get cheeky and snap back with a non-consequential response, expecting that their honesty means you have to spill.

    All you have to say is, "Oh, good for you!" and change the topic. If they don't get the message, refer to tip #3.

    See how you can respond—without answering—if you need to? Look, we spend about a third of our lives at work. Let's normalize asserting boundaries without

fear of consequences. There are always going to be people who make their own rules when it comes to skirting
civility or pushing boundaries. Luckily, you can push
back. It's okay to dodge unwanted questions. In fact, it's
a form of verbal self-defense—*shifting their force with
your power*—use it!

 ## Play Offense with Interruptions

Who could forget the infamous moment when Kanye
West jumped on stage at the 2009 Grammys and said, "I'm
gonna let you finish," stealing a monumental moment from
then-new-artist Taylor Swift? This moment perfectly dem-
onstrated something that many of us experience every day
in meetings and in our personal lives: being talked over and
interrupted.

See, "airtime" is a form of power. Not only does it feel
fairer on a team when we give everyone a chance to speak,
research has shown[1] that teams are actually more effective
when members make equal contributions to discussions.

But if you work with chronic interrupters and over-
talkers, how do you take matters into your own hands?
After all, doing nothing is hardly an option. When we don't
react to an everyday slight such as interruptions—it dimin-
ishes us and our contribution even further!

Here are five tactics you can use when you're interrupted
or talked over. This way, you can maintain your voice in
any conversation.

1. **Carry right on talking.** This is particularly important
   with a serial, repeat interrupter. With these interrupters,

it's more effective to continue speaking—which affirms your voice and contribution, rather than stopping, yielding, and giving your attention to the intrusion.

2. **Use your body.** The same tactic that works with my young twins when I'm on a call also works in business. If you're interrupted, as you carry on talking, try raising a hand to indicate, "Wait." You're issuing a physical signal to say, "I'm not finished." You can also "big up" your body when interrupted. If you're speaking seated, try standing up so you're more conspicuous.

3. **Speak slightly louder than the interrupter.** Susan Cain, author of *Quiet*, recommends that when you need to jump (back) into a crowded conversation that you "speak at a decibel level a little higher than the people around you." This also works well when you're interrupted. So if you were speaking let's say at a 6/10 in volume, increase to a 7/10. This unconsciously signals to the group that you're reclaiming your spot in the conversation—that you have something to say, and it's time to listen.

If interruptions are rampant, you can always make a nonjudgmental comment within your team. Keep it fact-based, as in, "That's the third time Neil got cut off" or "Everyone else has weighed in. I'm not finished." In these cases, you're citing observable behavior, not implying anything. This approach gives the interrupter a chance to correct what they're doing (in case they're somehow not aware of their behavior). Taking a stand quickly and succinctly helps you to speak your piece powerfully and address interruptions. That way you can move on to bigger, more meaningful things.

Look and See All the Feedback Opportunities

If someone asked me one of the top ways to build an excellent reputation—whether for an intern or an SVP—I'd say it's *asking for feedback*. Why?

Going after feedback, rather than waiting for it, makes you powerful. When we do this, we're not waiting, hoping, or wishing upon a star someone will share valuable data with us, we're initiating it. And we're that much closer to getting game-changing information we can incorporate into our plans. So how do we get started making this power move more often and owning more of our own growth and progress? Try these steps:

1. **Do some self-reflection of your own.** Think about the area you're interested in getting feedback on. Take some simple notes on where you're showing promise and what's gone well. Now look at things the other way. What skill, knowledge, or experience would enable you to make an even *bigger* difference? Have these notes prepared in advance of asking for feedback. They'll give you some easy-to-reference talking points and show the other person you've carefully considered your performance.

2. **Ask for balanced and specific feedback.** Learn from the mistake I made early on in my career: don't only ask for general feedback—because often, people will only give you the negative kind. Instead ask specifically for the good *and* the bad. After delivering a high-stakes presentation, for example, you could say to your

manager, "You just saw me present there. What's one thing that worked well and one thing I could do better next time?" It's just as important—if not more—to identify your strengths alongside your weaknesses.

3. **Make it bigger than you.** To encourage someone who's not forthcoming to give you straight feedback, try tying it to group performance rather than your individual performance. This way you can remind them of what's at stake more broadly. You can say, "I want all of us to be successful in our new product launch. Please tell me your thoughts on X, Y, and Z." Another way you could approach it is, "Our team really values your opinion, and I could use your help. Can you provide me with your feedback on ABC?"

Once you've heard feedback, thank the other person, clarify it if you need to, and contract to revisit the feedback on a future date to check in about your progress. I coach leaders that the first words out of their mouth after someone gives them feedback should be, "Thank you for sharing that with me." This not only encourages the feedback giver to do it again in the future, it acknowledges some of the bravery it took on their part to share it in the first place.

If there's something about the feedback you don't understand or agree with, probe for more information. Say, "Can you help me understand X better?" or "I really want to get a grasp of what you're saying. Can you share an example of a time I did ABC?"

As for contracting to revisit the feedback, you might close with something such as, "I want to work on this. Do you mind if I ask again after my next presentation to see how I've improved?"

Not all valuable feedback will land in your lap. By having an action plan for how you can go after feedback yourself, you'll get the unvarnished input you deserve. You'll build a reputation for being able to hear, and get better from, constructive criticism. Here's to feedback as fuel!

 ## Push Back on a Pushy Coworker

As a young consultant, I regularly attended meetings with a colleague named Dave. We were at the same level in our organization, helping our corporate clients work on employee engagement. But in front of clients, Dave would act like my boss. *Grrr.* He'd suggest that I do the "office housework" jobs such as scheduling and note-taking—something women of color are more likely to be asked to do[2]—while he nominated himself for high-stakes client presentations. Without fail, I'd end up leaving those meetings feeling worse about myself and mentally cursing Dave out. Can you say tiresome?!

If you work with a Dave of your own, don't worry—there are ways to address this power push and pull. Here are four strategies you can implement to be your own best self-advocate:

Prep Some Comebacks

Most of us don't do our best thinking on our feet, particularly if we're angry or frustrated. So when they say, "Here's how we're going to divvy up the work," you can be ready with, "That's one way to do it. I suggest we . . ." Or if they sign you up for a new initiative you don't want to be part of, say, "That's an interesting project. I'm not sure it's realistic with my workload though" or "Hmmm, let me talk to my manager about it."

Bring Your Sense of Humor

Consider taming your power-hungry colleague with something they're probably not expecting: levity. When they recommend you do the tedious work for the fourth time in a row, you could say, "Did I sign up for the grunt work and somehow forgot?" or "Thanks anyway, I'll take a pass" or "My answer is no, that is, if it's okay with you!"

Redirect Them

You can respect your own time, education, and level of experience by forwarding a pushy colleague elsewhere. If they're asking you to take on extraneous work, you can say, "Let me steer you to someone who knows more about that." Or redirect by saying no to an unwanted task such as scheduling the team dinner and offering a yes to something you do want to work on, such as writing the results report.

Get Air Cover

Yes, managers expect that you should be able to manage your time on your own. But your manager should be aware when you are being pulled in directions that prevent you from completing meaningful work. So ask your boss outright to provide cover. Inform them that you occasionally get asked to work on noncritical work and that you'd like to decline it. You can suggest that you'll check in with them when it's "on the line." Then ask them to back you up when you say no.

Having your self-esteem chipped away by a domineering colleague can be a total confidence vampire. Realize that by confidently standing up for yourself, you're combatting the toxic message that says it's better to settle and not make waves. No, it sure isn't! Setting clear limits will cement your reputation as someone who respects their own time, is thoughtful and reliable, and is looking for ways to add real value.

 ## Present Yourself to Big Wigs Like a Peer

There's an old saying I share with people over and over: *If you put somebody up on a pedestal, don't be surprised if they start to look down on you.*

And it's true, isn't it?

If we overfocus on hierarchy, we emphasize *their* position or clout, placing them *up there*, and putting ourselves *down here*. It becomes pretty easy to feel "less than."

As a recovering "good girl," I've definitely struggled with being overly deferential, particularly with authority figures. That strong psychological pull to be demure, yield, and make loads of space for them had me practically apologizing for the air I breathe.

That's why one of my go-to strategies for interacting with higher-ups now is to come at it partner to partner, or peer to peer. That's helped me drop certain behaviors such as thanking them excessively, saying "I'm sorry," or acting like a bother.

This has helped me make the shift toward signaling that *both of our times are valuable*, and practically speaking, it meant I started to act more like a fellow collaborator. This has required a switch in how I think about myself, how I carry myself, and how I treat the other person. I aim to be respectful but always on an equal plane—it doesn't matter if it's a recruiter, a client, or the president.

As you engage in conversations that are purposely peer-to-peer, try to create a confident, collaborative team feel. That essentially signals, "We're on the same team. It's you and I versus the problem." Removing hedging language such as "We could" or "We might" for more surefooted language also helps. You can lean on phrases such as "I recommend" or "Let's do XYZ" or "Based on running six end-to-end projects just like this, I think we ought to do X."

Here are some other *do's* and *don'ts* to handle this like a star:

Don't fawn:

- Instead of: "Thanks so much for meeting today and making time in your hectic schedule . . ."
- Say: "I'm so glad we could find a time to meet."

Don't hurry:

- Instead of: "I'm going to hurry through my list of questions here since I know you're busy . . ."
- Say: "I called this meeting so we can review five open questions together."

Don't apologize:

- Instead of: "Sorry, this last point isn't really important, so why don't we just go ahead and skip it."
- Say: "I'd like to look at one more point together before we finish."

Know this: you could be laid off, looking for work, stuck, or dissatisfied with your current job—and you're *still* worthy. Yep, it's a fact! Retire the need to defer and deny your power. Make the mental shift that you're an equal, and it'll translate to all kinds of upgrades.

 ## You're an Expert—Now Act Like It!

"Whatever you do, don't be the Cheesecake Factory of experts."

That's what my mentor told me when I was setting off to start my own business. His point was, don't try to be an expert in everything—if you want credibility, show people you know a lot about one overarching thing.

And it's enduring advice.

See, the Cheesecake Factory serves pasta, sushi, burgers, and more—and while that may grab plenty of people, it's hard to replicate that catchall approach as a respected professional. So how can you crystallize your specific gift, your niche?

Accept That You're *Already* an Expert

I mean it! Here's the thing. You are already a skilled, experienced go-to resource. You already have *the power*! To illustrate this, I'd like you to complete this sentence:

"I'm an expert in [your specific domain], focusing on [stylistic approach or important element you bring], which helps [cause/idea/mission] or reduces [problem/risk]."

For me, this sounds like: "I'm an expert in developing confident, awake leaders, who foster safety and belonging on their teams, which creates healthier, happier workplaces."

For Todd, it might sound like, "I'm a software developer with a passion for the human side of tech, which helps ensure that I create user-oriented solutions that matter."

Whether you're deep in your career niche, fresh out of college, starting your first job, or returning from time off to be a caregiver, it helps to complete this exercise. For someone who's returning to work after a leave period, it might look like:

"I'm an operations manager returning to the workforce, with expertise in improving quality, productivity, and efficiency across different industries. That helps business run smoothly!"

Your turn!

Now let's bring the expertise you've identified to life.

Use Your Story

The core of finding your voice is telling your own story. Start to practice talking about how your thinking evolved to get you where you are—or share a lightbulb moment, a struggle that became an eye-opener, even a happy accident that landed you where you are. Part of the unique thing you're bringing to the market is *you*, so get personal!

Be a Trend Spotter

Imagine yourself at a dinner party or in the boardroom, leading a conversation on your expertise. What are the forces and drivers that would add depth or important context to your points? Whether these are trends or research findings, think of them like the cone and sprinkles to your scoop of ice cream. They add structure, contrast, and interest. Is there something not being discussed in your world that should be? Start looking for trends, research, and movement there and weave that into your POV.

Don't Be so Modest

Don't overestimate what everyone else can do and underestimate what you do can do. Remember, *everybody is winging it*. Right now, try this little simulation with me: pretend you are the leading, foremost expert on . . . tobogganing. (Did I stress that you are truly the planet's top thinker on this?) Now, picture yourself on TV as a commentator, talking about the toboggan segment of the Winter Olympics. What does your confidence look like? Strong? Surefooted? Clear? Chances are, you're giving yourself permission to speak with a level of authority you don't typically give yourself.

The point is, it's time to stop thinking of yourself as a future expert. *You're an expert today.*

It's okay to be scared. Do it anyway. Get on a stage, write an article, apply for the job, nominate yourself for the leadership role. Endorse yourself, and other people will follow suit. Be the expert, and don't look back.

4 Release Overdoing, Overthinking, and Overexplaining

Have you ever taken on more than you can handle?

(If you're reading this, I bet you a million monopoly dollars the answer is yes!)

Maybe it was in an attempt to show you're a team player or that you're dedicated. Perhaps you felt less than good about your performance on one task and wanted to shine on a new one. Or it could be that you wanted to prove something to yourself: that you're smart and can do hard things!

If you've been guilty of overdoing it, you're not alone. Conventional career wisdom practically encourages it. The message we're given is: if you want to stand out at work, you need to raise your hand early and often, extend yourself cheerfully, and overdeliver. That way, you don't leave a speck of doubt in people's minds that you're capable, productive, and worthy.

Well, I have a different take. The habit of overdoing is noxious to your confidence. In fact, it's straight-up dangerous! See, when you require yourself to give "A++" effort or normalize overcommitting, you make overdoing the standard. That can create a work life governed by an equation where your self-worth corresponds to your productivity. And that hurts your confidence. It narrows your chances to succeed every day. And in some cases, sets an unmeetable norm. Ouch!

Here's one other red blinking caution light about over-functioning. When you overextend yourself, you exceed your own internal resources—mental, intellectual, physical—as though they can be borrowed from tomorrow, as if they were endlessly renewable. Of course, that's a fast-track to Burnoutville! It can also train other people to see you as "always on" and ready to say yes to whatever. And that's a reputation that can be hard to shake.

Overdoing can manifest as:

- Overcommitting: Volunteering to do something even when you don't need or want to do it
- Overanalyzing: Engaging in grueling rounds of mental analysis before you make a move or decision
- Overpreparing: Needing excessive preparation in order to trust yourself to rise to the moment
- Overexplaining: Articulating a point in excess, to avoid any semblance of uncertainty in your audience's minds

How to Get Unstuck from the "Over-delivery Trap"

On the other hand, "just enoughness"—my term for the *opposite* of over-functioning—helps you contribute and give value while maintaining your dignity. It requires restraint, mind you—knowing you *could* humanly push further if you had to, that you have the capacity to pitch in or come in early. "Just enoughness" means that most of the time you default to a pace and level of output that's doable and doesn't deplete you.

Striving for "very good" and "excellent," (rather than overdoing it), allows you to more fully embrace who you are and express it with confidence. Someone who's learning, who has strengths, faults, budding skills, vulnerabilities— who's okay with moving around the world in growth mode.

"Just enoughness" can manifest as:

- Negotiating deadlines or requests for more information in a way that suits your schedule and limits
- Stating a point and then letting it land, allowing for the possibility of intrigue, wonder, or questions from your audience
- Having a knowing confidence when you deliver reasonable value, choosing strategically where to give discretionary or extraordinary effort and attention
- Being willing to let your humanity and vulnerability show, not cultivating a work personality that's bulletproof

See how this keeps your own best interests front and center? How there's a sense of self-respect in curbing "overaction"?

And listen, it's totally normal if you feel nervous or apprehensive right now. You might be thinking, *I'm already known for always saying yes. What if it's too late to change that?* Or, *I'm so intimidated by my boss, I don't know how to maintain my boundaries.*

So let's get one thing straight: giving up the overdoing habit is totally doable. It doesn't matter if you overdeliver to prove your superpowers to the world, as a form of defiance, or even to self-punish (again, ouch!). Regardless, a big part of starting this freeing transformation is realizing this: overdoing takes up your limited precious, everyday energy—and *gives it to the wrong things*. When we over-rationalize, overkill, overanalyze, and overdo, we are not living our lives with any kind of equilibrium!

How do I know?

Well, like I've told you, I'm a recovering "good girl." Aka over-functioner . . . and people pleaser. For years, I felt the word "yes!" tumbling out of my mouth in answer to all kinds of requests before I could even think them through. (I once told my boss I'd work while on a romantic getaway with my husband. Gah! More on that later in this chapter.) But being indiscriminate with what I agreed to was tiring and, after a while, stoked my resentment. (I'd also guess that it caused me to grow my company at least 50% slower because overcommitting stole my focus.) Thank goodness for patient therapists and business coaches—and family and friends who love you enough to question why you're doing so much, giving something away for free, or treating your time like it doesn't matter.

Today I'm happily done with the idea that I constantly need to justify or strain myself to be adequate. I've found the upshot to "just enoughness" is realizing I can deploy my energy graciously, with thought and consideration, *on my terms*. I do not, I repeat, do not, need to give all my power to the other person. Not just that, but I've realized that every good thing, including rest, does not need to be earned.

In this chapter, I'll show you, too, how to develop the kind of self-trust that lets you move from thinking to action. Whether with your mindset, your body, or through your interactions, *you* can find that lovely, reassuring place called "good enough." It's where you know how to make momentum happen, where you know when to quit a faulty course, where you actively challenge the blanket thought that "if one completed task is good, then 100 must be great." And yep, it feels fantastic!

So many people don't experience the freedom of confidence because there's a big, hairy, blue monster standing in their way. What's that monster's name? Fear! Specifically, fear they are inadequate. Most people relate to this fear on some level, so you and I both know how painful it is.

When you reprogram your need to outdo, you create a new set point for success, one where you recognize the delight of adequacy. It's time to start appreciating what you already have, do, and contribute. And to let go of the wearisome burdens of excess you don't need to carry. Let's get at it!

You Don't Owe Anyone an (Over) Explanation

Last fall, a fellow parent at Little League soccer asked me if I had the bandwidth to coach my son's team.

I drew in an exhausted breath.

To say that the coming semester was a busy time for me as a speaker, business owner, and mom is an understatement. But rather than directly saying, "Coaching isn't possible for me this year," I found myself giving a long-winded explanation about the 33 things happening in my life that would make coaching hard.

It wasn't eloquent. In fact, I knew almost immediately that I *overdid* my words and *under-delivered* my message. "*Selena, that's enough!*" my mind pleaded. But the over-explanation train had left the station, and I was its passenger.

Have you ever been there?

Over-explaining is a nervous habit, and it's one that comes from fear: Fear of delivering a message that could sound harsh. Fear of taking a strong position that isn't 100% bulletproof. Fear of not making sense. Fear of people thinking your idea is foolish.

The trouble with over-explaining is that it *weakens your words*. And you know what else? It *dilutes* your message!

The next time you feel the urge to explain—then explain some *more*—use these strategies to regain your poise and confidence:

1. **Keep it succinct.** When you feel the urge to over-explain, pause and breathe. Then briefly provide your answer to the request. You could even say, "Can you give me a minute to think about it?" to give yourself a moment to gather your thoughts. Remember, you do not need to justify your position. If an explanation is absolutely necessary, keep it brief—two or three sentences maximum. Oftentimes, the more elaboration we give, the more we create openings for the other person to start negotiating with us! So keep it decisive, firm, and most of all, short.

2. **Sit with the discomfort of others**. Letting people down is part of life! You might feel crummy telling someone

no, but you can't live your life without ever disappointing folks. When you say no, you can empathize with any rejection they may feel without becoming the rescuer of their situation. So embrace the fact that not everyone's needs will be met by you. And here's a bonus tip: People may feel negatively toward you when you assert your boundaries. Expect and anticipate their resistance—see it as part of the "stuff" of standing up for yourself and not a sign that you did anything wrong.

Breaking the over-explaining habit is a huge boon to your professional and personal life. Successful and contented people have good boundaries—that's how they're able to perform well!

And I'm happy to tell you this: keeping it short and sweet gets easier with time. The cherry on top? People will notice, appreciate, and follow your example.

 ## Get out of Your Head

If there's one thing overthinkers have in common, it's a tendency to ignore or overlook the physical cues coming from our bodies. Think about it: when you're busy shuffling your thoughts over and over like a deck of cards, it's hard to tune into—let alone regulate—your body! That matters because research[1] has shown that overthinking can exacerbate depression, increase negative thinking, and impair problem solving.

I've noticed that I'm especially likely to overthink after leaving a party or large social situation. Afterward, I run through every interaction in my mind "to make sure it was okay."

Now, if left unbridled, I can stay on that internal tread-mill for hours. Yikes—can you say exhausting? The good news is I've found ways to stop living in my head so much at moments like this and to tune into my body to pivot that energy. These techniques can work for you too. Try them out to stop ruminating and engage your body in a positive way:

1. **Use the stop-clap technique.** When enough is enough with your thoughts, try the stop-clap technique. To do this, I want you to picture a red stop sign in your mind and then immediately clap your hands as a way to break with what you were just thinking and tune in to the present moment. This works best for me when I clap loudly. It interrupts the mental pattern I was just in and helps me start *fresh*.

2. **Try box breathing.** When you "box-breathe," you help return your breathing to a normal rhythm. This is a great way to tune into your body and release your 90-mile-per-hour thought pattern. To do this, (1) exhale to a count of four, (2) then hold your lungs empty for a four-count, (3) now inhale to a count of four, and (4) last, hold your lungs for a count of four before exhaling. Repeat, and you'll be better off, mentally and physically, for it.

3. **Visualize a different reaction.** Think about a situation where you're likely to overthink—like a one-on-one with your boss or a meeting series with an intimidat-ing work colleague. How would your most evolved self, or best version of you, navigate that stressful situation? Mentally, I want you to picture it. Using my earlier example, my best self would leave a party, think, or talk through a couple of highlights and then *let it go*.

Conjuring that image of my preferred reaction really helps me—it gives me an aspiration to *embody* next time. What is it for you?

Stopping the overthinking habit might seem like a private thing, but I have news for you: it translates to your outer actions too, such as how you carry yourself, what you choose to engage in or sit out of—or when you speak up or stay quiet. But you are not stuck. You are the leader you've always been waiting for. You can actively steer your inner overthinker in a positive direction. Jump in the driver's seat, and *let's go*!

 ## Are You a Victim or Creator?

"*He* made me mad."
"*They* hurt my feelings."
"*She* is holding me back."
Have you ever gotten caught in a mental loop like this? I know I have. These phrases can overestimate everyone else's role and leave you feeling resigned and powerless. That's because when they're repeated like a mantra, they keep you in the mindset of a victim. Victims blame, complain, make excuses, and repeat behavior. When I was younger, I didn't realize I had a victim mindset.

(Note, I'm not talking about victims of violence. Some people are victims of violence, and it is not their fault. I'm talking about people who feel like victims of circumstances they have the power to change.)

On the other hand, when you think with a creator mindset, you take responsibility and action. You seek solutions. You turn complaints into requests or plans. You create a new path forward.

So how do we make this switch in real life? Here are some examples of what I'm talking about:

Instead of: "I failed my accounting course because she's a terrible instructor," try: "You know what? I wasn't well prepared for the test. Here's how I'll study differently next time . . ."

Instead of: "My boss is giving me the most boring projects on earth; they put me to sleep!" try: "I'm going to propose to my boss I either come off a useless project or get assigned to a new one."

Instead of: "My team is totally unmotivated. I've tried everything and, believe me, nothing works," try: "I haven't figured out yet what motivates my team. I'm going to consult with some other colleagues about what I could do."

Instead of: "I get no recognition, I feel invisible," try: "I'm going to prepare a proposal for my boss suggesting my title and level of oversight are expanded."

See the difference? Try to shift your helpless statements in this same way, and then complement them with these techniques:

- **Put things in their right compartments.** Research shows that part of the negative victim experience is pervasiveness. Victims assume that failure in one area of life equates to failure in life overall. But creators tend to *compartmentalize* their helplessness to one area of life. So next time you have a helpless tape playing in your head, write down your stream of consciousness and then actually put it in a box (or another compartment). You can always revisit it later, but doing this creates a powerful physical cue for your brain to stop the negativity.

- **Summon the progress principle.** When you or someone else struggles with feelings of helplessness, you can use a wonderful tool called the progress principle.[2] Researchers found that simply making progress on meaningful work led subjects to greater motivation and happiness. So, as you support yourself or your teammates and leaders through their helpless moments, try to focus on reminding them how far they've come.

Remember, you are not helpless in the face of catastrophizing. The opposite of learned helplessness is learned experimentation, optimism, and determination. Keep that in mind when you need to shift from a victim to creator mindset.

Remember, you get to choose—and create—what's next. Create something great.

 ## Treat Your Comparison-itis

There you are, plugging along on a regular old workday. You're feeling pretty good. Slowly but surely, chipping away at the work task in front of you. Then, needing a quick little break, you jump for a minute onto Instagram.

And then you do it.

You compare yourself to a friend or colleague who has more influence, "juice," salary, fitness, or [fill in the blank] than you.

And now you feel heavy. Deflated. Down.

So often, comparison leaves us feeling bad. It robs us of feeling proud of our gifts. And here's the thing: the comparisons that we get hooked on—that leave us feeling crappy—are big *energy vampires* that we can't afford to indulge.

Next time you're tempted to overdo it comparing yourself with someone else, consider these alternatives. They'll
invigorate you, boost your confidence, and help you get
back on track.

1. *Physically remove yourself from triggering comparisons.*
   Social comparison bias is when we make upward comparisons, where we compare ourselves to others who
   seem better off than us—and it's been shown to lead
   to self-destructive behavior. Negative coping skills can
   range from increased substance use, eating disorders,
   alcoholism, and more. But here's the great news: you
   can actively limit your exposure to images or social
   media feeds that make you feel lousy. So be cautious of
   your use! While you're at it . . .

2. *Unfollow and unsubscribe from people who make you feel
   badly, and/or disconnect from them IRL (in real life).* It
   may sound simple, but don't expose yourself to people,
   TV shows, or social media sites when you are already
   feeling low. You can also set aside part of a day to audit
   who you follow so that you're seeing posts that invigorate and inspire you. Similarly, consider who makes you
   feel lousy after you're around them and edit them from
   your routines.

3. *Admire the beauty of others, but avoid comparing yourself to anyone else.* When you engage, physically, in the
   comparison game, you can create a world where you're
   not quite where you want to be and where everyone
   else seems to have been dealt a better hand or is further
   ahead. When this urge crops up, put a rubber band on
   your wrist and lightly snap it! It's simple but effective.
   Of course, you can enjoy and compliment others on

their beauty, but creating that side-by-side appraisal of them versus you is unnecessary and usually unhelpful.

4. *Start a wave of appreciation.* After a particularly tough week of body image doldrums, I decided it was time to turn the page and shift my mindset. I ended up writing a top-ten list of things I like about myself. It was silly and fun—but you know what? It changed the negative momentum for the better. Take out a piece of paper right now and come up with 10 things you appreciate and like about your body, your mind, your job, your family, whatever—I guarantee a mood boost after doing this!

Unburdening yourself from comparison starts with saying no to negative or berating self-talk. It's also about creating positive moments every day where you cultivate real appreciation for yourself. So don't overvalue what others bring to the table and undervalue what you bring. Start a wave of appreciation in yourself today!

 ## Drop the Filler Words

Did you ever have a meaningful moment in your career when you stammered and staggered to get out the right words? While your brain was (over)thinking about what to do next, your lips were probably making sounds like "Uh," "Um," and "So . . ."

When we're unsure or overanalyzing, these filler words can be difficult to shake (and can get out of control). Now let me be clear: it's no big deal when they're said once or twice in a meeting (in which case they can actually make a person seem more considered), it's their *repetitive* use that really hurts a person's credibility.

When we hear consistent verbal stumbling, such as "Um-ing" and "Uh-ing," we assume the speaker is struggling to improvise or unsure of themselves.

The good news is you can steer your speech habits away from "Um" and "Uh" to more surefooted language. Try experimenting with the following strategies to reduce these words in your speech:

1. *Hear yourself out loud.* Sometimes firsthand experience is the greatest teacher. If you listen to a recording of a conference call where you regularly say "Uh," you may have a full-body cringe. Ack, I know, but this instant feedback and reality check are really important steps in letting go of filler words. An added bonus: once you hear yourself filling silence with "Uh," you will begin noticing when other people do it too. Use your observations as a listener and speaker to let this habit go. Start by getting out that video camera to record a presentation or listen to an audio recording of a recent call. Face the music. Remember, you can't change what you don't acknowledge.

2. *Preplan your transitions.* One of the functions of "um" is to tell your audience you're not done talking yet and need to gather your thoughts. As an alternative, have some transitions ready to use in any presentation or meeting. This has been transformational for me as a public speaker. Now I use transitions such as "Let's move on to . . .," "Another important consideration is. . .," or even "Let's transition to talking about . . ." Practicing these go-to transitions will begin to feel natural and will lessen your dependence on "Um."

3. *Chunk your information.* One thing is for sure—we're most likely to engage in waterfall speech or rambling when we're overthinking on the spot. Presentation trainer Olivia Mitchell recommends chunking your sentences ahead of speaking them and then leaving a pause. Says Mitchell, "When you chunk, you get into a rhythm: burst of words/break/burst of words/break . . . Focus on that rhythm and your 'Ums' will go." So try to address one issue per chunk. An example would be chunk 1: "For the campaign launch, we'll do X." Chunk 2: "For the campaign marketing email, we'll do Y". Chunk 3: "For the launch event, we'll do Z."

Remember, meetings are a kind of ongoing audition for our jobs. It's a daily opportunity to remind people of our experience and value. So make sure you're giving your words the weight and importance they deserve. With greater awareness, a commitment to not overthink, and self-compassion (always!), the "Ums" will lessen—I promise.

Deem Yourself Decisive

Have you ever been stuck in a group where people can't make up their mind about what to get for lunch? It's a small—even trivial—decision, and yet the conversation feels circular and never ending! This same indecision happens all the time in the workplace.

As common as it is for people to waffle and waver, one way to start to command more authority is to be decisive. Because the truth is, indecision is a form of decision—and not a strong one. So if your goal is to make bold bets—to step up and lead—indecision won't be the vehicle to get you there.

To help with this, here are four small habits to be more decisive—and really claim some of that up-for-grabs power in many daily interactions:

1. **Start small.** If being decisive is foreign to you, practice making small decisions in your life—with some constraints. For example, decide in 40 seconds what you'll wear today, then follow through. (I'm serious. Set a timer and stick to it.) By repeating this in small, time-limited ways and following through with your decisions, you'll build your comfort for making bigger decisions quickly.

2. **Check it against your vision.** It's much easier to be decisive if you have a clear vision for the future. If, as a finance director, your vision is to foster a department that delivers accurate information, improves transparency, and promotes innovation, then you essentially have a compass for whether your decision is on- or off-course. Keep updating your long-term vision— it'll only help you think clearly and accurately as a decision-maker.

3. **Use informed gut instinct.** The truth is, you will almost always work with imperfect or incomplete information. Accept this reality. That way, you can use what you do have: your past experiences and observations— and your gut sense of what's right. Scan past events, experiences, and precedents you've observed for whether your decision is sound. You can ask yourself, *Based on what I know, what's the worst that can happen and what's the best that can happen?* Then check your gut instinct or immediate sense of what's right.

4. **Make a public commitment.** Realize a good decision is, well, good enough! It's okay when it doesn't feel absolutely perfect or bulletproof. When you've used the quick checks we've walked through, you're ready to make a public commitment with confidence. Use decisive—not watered down—wording such as, "I'll vouch for X," "I recommend we go with option A," or "I'm ready to commit to Y." Making this public commitment increases others' comfort and their trust in you as someone who's thought things through and arrived at a sound conclusion.

As you put yourself out there, don't waver unnecessarily. Even if it feels as if it'll protect you from being vulnerable or exposed, true confidence comes from making hard decisions and then backing them. Remember, a wrong decision is usually less catastrophic than indecision. So prepare to be wrong sometimes—you can totally handle it! Go forth anyway.

Putting your support behind your decision is putting support behind yourself. Trust the wealth of knowledge and experience you've built up. And when it comes to making big decisions, remember, *everyone is winging it.*

 ## Shrink Your Output

Someone once asked me about what it was like to write a book. My joking response: "I had a really clean house." In my case, the daunting task of writing so many words from my home office made me want to get up and do anything else but write. You know, like straightening up little messes. Sorting through my closet. Or trying my hand at a complex

Norwegian cake recipe! (It turned out pretty good, but it sure didn't help my writing!) Here's the thing though—there's a better way to tackle big, intimidating projects than just overstressing or avoiding them.

That better way is through micro to-dos. This means breaking down large, daunting tasks into smaller, more manageable ones. That matters because when people learn to set realistic and smaller goals, research shows they can actually achieve *more*. Counterintuitive, right? But here's what else is really encouraging: People who make their goals smaller feel happier in the process—and who wouldn't sign up for that! Let's look at three ways to apply this concept to our own lives.

1. **Shrink the size of your goal.** Jon Acuff, author of *Finish: Give Yourself the Gift of Done*,[4] has a clear prescription—and I think you're going to like it! He suggests as a rule to "cut your goal in half." So, for example, let's say you've been cowering in fear at your to-do item to "Start the Market Research Project." It's a large, complex project and you feel like you don't know where to start. Rather than attempting to "Start the Market Research Project," your task could become "Build the market research project timeline." See what we did there? We shifted a large, ambiguous undertaking and halved it into a smaller, concrete task we could start right away.

2. **Try the Pomodoro method.** Developed by productivity expert Francesco Cirillo, this is a time management approach where you break your workday into 25-minute chunks, separated by five-minute breaks. The idea is that you pick a task that needs to get done.

Then you set a timer for 25 minutes and commit to doing *only that task* for the whole time. By making your time blocks small—only 25 minutes—you have a more manageable goal. Pomodoro also works because it applies some pressure on us to get things done right now, not later. (It has the added benefit of giving your brain and body regular breaks. If I'd used five-minute breaks to sort my closet, I'd have had an organized closet and a book more quickly!)

3. **Sandwich your "Pomodoros," or micro to-dos, with small breaks.** When you're in the middle of a period of "doing," anticipating an upcoming break can be an incentive to complete your task. But taking breaks can also clear and sharpen your mind. These micro breaks—defined as being 30 seconds to 5 minutes long—should *not* be work related! You can get up and walk around, text a buddy, visit a colleague, or stretch in your chair. Or if you're like me, you can find your next snack. And breaks? They don't just feel good, they actually reboot your brain. Just one break improves your mental acuity by 13%.

Whittling down the size of your working sessions or goals may not always feel natural. But it's a great technique for jumping in and starting something. As I write this book today, giving myself little writing "sprints" (rather than expecting marathons) has been freeing and productive. Whether you're completing a small project or finishing something that feels as big as a book, by making your goals manageable you'll achieve more—and you'll feel more satisfied. Now it's time for you to go after a micro to-do. Remember, think big but start small.

Set Clear Limits

Have you ever worked with someone who had boundary issues? Maybe they overdid the word "yes." Maybe they deferred their own needs to those of others.

It can be hard to watch, right?

I know because I used to be one of these people. I can remember being so dedicated to saying yes to every project that I worked through the first vacation my husband and I took as newlyweds. And guess what? Even though we lucked out on a beautiful hotel room with a stunning view of Seattle, I couldn't enjoy it because . . . *work*! I learned my lesson *big time* on that trip and yep, I'm happy to report I haven't done it again.

Look, boundaries aren't just a work thing—they're those psychological and emotional—even physical guardrails—that keep us safe. They communicate to the world where we've set up limits and where we're comfortable existing. If you're a little too good at saying yes or feel pressure to be overly agreeable, here are some concrete ways you can skill up in setting clear limits:

- ***Identify a limit of yours that's either loose or nonexistent and causing discomfort.*** It might be that you regularly leave work later than you plan to, so you're chronically late for school pickup.

   Maybe it's that you say yes to unreasonable deadlines whenever a certain person asks you. Maybe you regularly attend a meeting series where you're just not needed or adding value.

   You can't change what you don't label. So right now, jot down one boundary you can strengthen. Now add an action you'll put into place to honor that boundary. It might be: Take a 20-minute lunch break rather than working through lunch.

- *Communicate your boundaries.* You might contract verbally with your partner that you'll leave work at 5 p.m. no matter what.

  You can tell your team you're opting out of certain meetings with the next department and that you appreciate them providing cover and backing your decision.

  Take a moment to identify who you can share your boundary with, in your personal or work network, so you can strengthen it. Jot it down and encourage this person to hold you accountable.

- *Be willing to say no when your boundary's being infringed.* Say you're feeling physically lousy—like you might come down with a cold. A request pops up for you to travel on a last-minute work trip. You entertain going anyway, but your gut says, "Don't."

  Honoring your boundary means sharing directly, "No. I can't." It doesn't mean saying, "I *could*, but I'd rather not." Remember, "No" can be a complete thought.

  You don't need to go into lengthy explanations. Don't pull a "Selena at the soccer game" and overexplain your reasoning! If you must, one simple reason supporting your "No" is often enough.

- *Mentally scan the environment where you work.* While our own boundaries matter, we also need to have our eyes open if there's a mismatch between us and our work environment. What does your work culture promote? What's the approach on your team to people's personal boundaries?

If your boss is a workaholic, for example, or you're in a job or company that constantly violates the boundaries you communicate, it might be time to leave.

Sure, we need to compromise at times, but it's not okay if there's constant disregard for your boundaries.

Setting boundaries can feel nerve-wracking, awkward— even scary. But as someone who used to avoid it, I can tell you the good news is it gets easier with practice. Experiment with putting limits down. Make some mistakes as you go, and be compassionate and forgiving of yourself when they happen. Start where you are now, and you'll be amazed how quickly things change!

 ## Do Beauty Checks

Here's a hard truth about overthinking, overdoing, overanalyzing, and overcommitting:

Life is already hard enough.

Life will throw dozens of fresh challenges your way. Plenty of them unforeseen. Some of these will be annoying. But some of them will be *agonizing*.

Are you really going to live your life piling on top of that pain and discomfort?

Right! *It's a hard no.*

This is where the concept of beauty checks comes in. I met Dr. Lisa Moscoso, division chief and professor at Washington University School of Medicine, while we were teaching up-and-coming physicians about leadership. Dr. Moscoso's focus was on well-being and resilience; she shared that even during her own challenging life moments, she started a practice of becoming intentional about taking time to recognize the beauty all around her.

This everyday habit—which she encourages learners to adopt—becomes especially important during times of real adversity. So how can you stop the suffering caused by overdosing on stress and self-doubt and start doing more beauty checks?

By shifting your perspective and seeking out the positive. Instead of being a heat-seeking missile looking for threats and hazards, you can thoughtfully start to notice what's beautiful and worthy of appreciation. How?

- **Find one beautiful thing now.** All around us, right this minute, there is beauty everywhere. If you are attentive, you will see it. So get in the mindful habit—wherever you are—of finding *one beautiful thing*. It could be something you see, smell, or feel—or something that's not even in your eyesight right now. Go ahead and conjure that in your mind and senses. For me, I'm picturing the littlest, cutest freckles my daughter gets on her rosy cheeks in the summer. This year, I started to build on this practice by taking a photo each day of one beautiful thing! For someone else, it might be the lovely smell of being freshly showered and clean—or putting your eyes on the most plump, beautiful fruit growing in your garden. Or it might be a shared moment cackling loudly with a good friend. Play the beautiful movie in your head and let yourself feel it deeply!

- **Appreciate your booboos.** Chances are, you've had stumbles and disappointments and dashed expectations. It's part of the good ol' human package! Sometimes our pain is like an alert system telling us something's wrong—and giving us the chance to deal with it.

Sometimes our pain is just there and impossible to override. As you take stock of some of your own challenges, I want you to think of three situations where your scar from a challenge—mental or physical—was a great teacher or important part of your learning. Where you grew in spite of that trial. Immediately, this makes me think of a time I sent an audition tape to an online education company. More than 12 producers gave me back unvarnished, hard-hitting critical feedback about my delivery. I nearly melted into a puddle of horror as I read it. I felt exposed, naked, and embarrassed about my foibles. But that journey taught me all kinds of lessons about presenting and connecting with audiences and helped me get at least 50% better! Plus, the company ended up bringing me on. How about you? Was it a training or degree you persevered through? A time you got challenging feedback and ran with it? A commitment to your family? A scary brush with your health that made you appreciate your life?

By checking your overstress at the door, you can start to notice more often what's beautiful and worthy of appreciation. That grows your resiliency skills and empowers you to see what's positive, what's working, what's beautiful!

5 Negotiate Your Success

Negotiating for what you need can change the course of your life.

How do I know?

Just like a lot of teenagers, I had big dreams to go to college. I knew it wouldn't be easy for my family to afford—after all, I have three older siblings! But my parents always told me, "Selena, we'll find a way."

Well, very suddenly when I was thirteen, my father passed away.

We were . . . *I was* devastated. And from that time onward, with my mom working as a nurse, and picking up not just one job but two, we struggled financially.

As college loomed closer, I applied to schools and got accepted to one I was really excited about. That university gave me some financial aid, and my mom was insistent we'd scrape together to cover the rest. (If any of you have a single mom, you know they are the *masters* of doing a lot with a little!)

Well, I went to freshman year at college and I *loved* it. But when I got the financial aid letter for year two, lo and behold, the aid dollars were much smaller. Ooof.

My mom sat me down at the kitchen table and with pain in her eyes, said, "Honey, I can't swing it this time. I can't send you back"

Whoa. I realized in that moment that if anyone was going to change the course of things, it had to be *me*. My mom had never been to a four-year college, let alone haggled with one!

So, 18-year-old me sat down and typed up a lengthy appeal of the financial aid package. I offered to be of service to the university as a student worker, a tour guide, a cafeteria worker, anything. I included all the ways I wanted to add to the student community, too. I pushed back and asked them to keep me there.

To my happy shock, they increased the financial aid package. Not just for year two, but for year three and four, also. And they gave me all those student jobs too!

What I realized then was that asking for what you need can *alter the course of your life*. Whether you feel confident asking is beside the point—because asking is how you *build* confidence. Did I feel confident writing that appeal letter? Not particularly. But the fact that I can tell this story today in past tense, because results came of it, is the best kind of reward. Even when you have loved ones, mentors, or allies who support you, no one else can ask on your behalf the way *you* can. You have to be your own number one advocate!

Whether it's more money, a flexible work arrangement— even a commuter benefit—most of us can agree that asking is a powerful tool to get these things. But for so many people, the process can spur different kinds of apprehension.

Lots of times we overestimate someone's else's power and underestimate our own value. Or another challenge I see, having trained thousands of professionals on negotiating, is a fear of damaging the relationship by making an assertive request.

How about for you?

Can you relate to wanting more but hesitating to ask for it?

Here's what's encouraging: negotiating for what we want and need is a process of trying, experimenting, and seeing what works. Not every negotiation is going to play out like it does on TV or like the best version in your head. That's okay! Those losses actually matter as much as your wins. They teach you about what influences other people (or doesn't!) and they deepen your sense of your own values.

And what's more? You're not starting at zero as a negotiator. As a professional, you negotiate all the time. To satisfy your clients and customers, to advocate for the right approach on a project, or to get the buy-in of an internal business partner. But my guess is that you don't always see this as negotiating. You probably think of it as *managing it, handling it,* or *getting it done.*

My question for you is, what if you brought that same ferocious advocacy you bring to serving your customers, peers, and direct reports to those areas that benefit *you*? Like your work assignments, that brand-new, amazing role at your company that doesn't yet exist? And how about for work-life boundaries, or if someone makes you feel small?

You might also want to negotiate for structural changes at your company such as salary transparency, more inclusive benefits, or more urgent action around promoting diverse leadership.

One of my hopes in offering you this how-to chapter is for you to claim credit for the many ways you *already* use this skill so you come at these conversations even more strategically and so you negotiate even more often.

Because the thing is, negotiating for what you need, and holding firm if you don't get it, is one of the best ways to be authentic. Speaking your needs doesn't just empower you, it gives the other person a chance to solve your pain or discomfort. It's really a form of open communication!

As you test out the techniques in this chapter—and string together your own set of lessons or "pearls," remember this: nearly everything is discussable, is figure-outable, is something you can revise or adapt by making your needs clear. Very little is written in stone and off-limits. So stop settling for *less than optimal* and start looking for those powerful win-wins, starting now.

 ## Don't Tell Yourself No before They Do

Once upon a time I was part of a work team that had a standing meeting at 6:30 p.m. on Thursdays.

I hated it!

I am fiercely protective of my weeknights. I have young twins and a husband I want to spend time with, plus I love upcycling old furniture, my TJ Maxx shopping habit, and building biceps while I listen to comedy podcasts. Like most of us, I badly need time off the clock to feel like me.

Despite hating this commitment, I continued to show up at 6:30 feeling annoyed and resentful—before, after, and during meetings.

After nearly a year of stewing, I finally decided to speak up. When I did, and I proposed switching to a meeting time that was within everyone's workday (the team spanned three time zones), people quickly said yes.

Wait, whaaaat?! It was that easy to get what I wanted.

So what took me so long to advocate for myself?

I was telling myself no before they did. I continued to say yes to an unwelcome commitment, and it was like saying a loud, screaming no to myself the whole time.

What I learned that day is that you don't have to settle for less than great in your life. This means being the chief negotiation officer of your time and energy.

It's one of the best ways to build your confidence and self-esteem because it reinforces that you're a capable grown-up who can effect change. Try these mindset shifts and mantras as you go:

1. "It's not my job to decide if it's a *no*." When we preempt others' rejection with our own, we don't give ourselves a chance to get to the bargaining table (let alone persuade them!). Remind yourself that the spark in you that wants to make a worthwhile request has already cleared the bar.

2. "I just need to take one step toward action." Rather than focus on *not doing* something—aka avoiding—focus on *doing*. What's one next step you could take today to further your proposal? For example, researching fair compensation rates or speaking to your network.

3. "I have a high degree of self-agency." This phrase reminds me I am the number one agent of change in

my career and life, and the same is true for you. Instead of putting all the focus on *them*, focus on the fact that nothing will progress without your *self-directed* action.

It sounds simple, and it is. With practice, you'll learn to accept fears of "what they might think of me," and go forth and advocate for what you need anyway.

Of course, it doesn't mean you'll always get what you want. My team could've insisted on keeping the 6:30 meeting time, and then I would've had to make some decisions. But you miss 100% of the shots you don't take.

Start now to create a powerful cascade in your life: say *yes* to yourself.

 ## Make Friends with LARA

Think about a time you summoned the nerve to make a request—even a little one—but then your request got denied or rejected. Did that response make you want to slink out of the room or evaporate? Did you feel tempted right afterward to say, "Let's just forget we ever had this little talk!"?

If that sounds like you, I want to introduce you to someone named LARA. Okay, it's not a *someone* exactly but a powerful framework for dealing with other people's resistance. It can open up and improve communication and help you and the other person find a shared understanding.

Developed at Stanford University,[5] LARA stands for: *Listen, Affirm, Respond, and Ask Questions.*

So how does this look in real life? Well, let's say you're proposing a new role that's really needed in your department. You've presented an overview of the role to your manager, justification supporting it, and shown how you could bring valuable skills to the role.

Your manager starts to mutter some fuzzy points about their discomfort. What can you do? This is an opportune moment to use LARA!

- **Listen:** You start out by listening to their perspective. I don't just mean tuning in generally, I mean generously listening with your whole body: feet, hips, and shoulders squared to the person speaking. Your eyes are chiefly focused on them, not looking at competing screens or out the conference room window. And of course, your ears are listening intently, taking in the substance and tone of what they're saying. As you do this, you set aside your own agenda. You make that person feel like there is no one else in the world you need to attend to at the moment but them.

- **Affirm:** Next, you affirm the other person. This way, you're validating they have an opinion on the matter and you've heard them—even if you disagree with it. So think about a feeling or value you share with the speaker. You might say, "I hear you saying this role feels really new and different. I can appreciate that." When we affirm a person, rather than rushing to defend our stance, it throws them a little bone that says, "I get your discomfort." Other examples might include "I appreciate your honesty" or "I sense we both care a lot about X." That helps you come across as reasonable, openminded, and cooperative.

- **Respond:** After you affirm the other person, it's time to answer their concerns or questions directly. What supporting evidence or added insight can you share to address their resistance? Or how can you share trends,

or a benchmark or metric that's convincing? Be creative as you respond to their fears or concerns. Using
our example of proposing a new role, you might say,
"Here's the good news, this role is very similar—in
many ways—to a newer role that's been created one
department over/at a competitor's company, and from
what I understand, that position has been a big success." And if you don't have the information you need
to address their concerns immediately, that's okay, too!
(Remember from the last chapter, you don't need to
constantly over-prepare!) You can say, "I understand
your concern, and I'm going to research how other
companies have handled it and get back to you." This
shows you're committed to making the role work.

- **Ask questions:** This is all about deepening the dialogue so you're not staying on the surface of the
  conversation, but you're getting to the core of what's
  creating a block. If your boss counters your response
  with, "Well, I'm pretty sure we can't create new roles
  midyear," you could open up the dialogue more by
  asking some open-ended, diagnostic questions. For
  example: "Can you help me understand how new roles
  are greenlit?" or "What would need to be true for you
  to be comfortable moving forward?" or "What else
  could I share with you about the other role that would
  be helpful?"

LARA is a great way to practice empathy and curiosity.
It honors the fact that everyone's perspective is unique. It
can also do wonders to help you negotiate win-win solutions you never even dreamed of.

Exercise Silence

In the summer of 2021, I posted a video on social media, not giving it much deep thought or afterthought. In it, I acted out some powerful ways to use silence in a negotiation. That Friday, while I was at a bouncy place with my son, my social media manager, Madyn, called me. My post was climbing its way to 1.3 million views!

There's a reason this video went viral and struck a nerve. For one, choosing to be silent—in a strategic way—seems like the very last thing we should do in a negotiation. Isn't it too passive of a move—or worse, awkward?

In fact, when someone gives us an unsatisfactory answer (as in "No, I won't be recommending you for a promotion this year"), we have a juicy peach of a moment to engage in silence. Silence can work well as an initial response to big news, when a lot has been said and we need to think or when we disagree. It also buys you time to collect your thoughts about what to do or say next.

By engaging in silence, with a resting neutral face (RNF), the pocket of quiet we're creating can be perceived by the other person as a leveling of power. Not just, that, but the other person will often feel a need to fill the silence. For example, your counterpart may share a piece of information you didn't know but needed.

The other great thing is if you tend to feel pressure to be agreeable or deferential, inserting moments of quiet can help you go more slowly and be strategic about your reactions. That makes you less likely to nod in agreement or say, "Okay" if in fact you hate what you're hearing.

Here are the two most important moments to use it in a negotiation:

- **Moment 1: Right after you make a request.** Let's say you've just made your case for getting a raise. You've laid out your reasoning and clearly made your request. This is the time to be quiet! That way, you don't start adding more words out of nervousness that lesson your request such as, ". . . if you can afford it" or ". . . but I know this has been a rough year for the company." Instead, give yourself at least seven seconds of silence to let your request land and to show that you stand behind it. And yes, I definitely recommend counting to seven—slowly—in your head!

- **Moment 2: Right after they respond.** When your counterpart answers you, whether with a qualm or in agreement, at least initially, again engage in some brief silence. Mind you, this isn't an icy stare, nor is it an air of indifference; instead it's as though you're mulling things and not rushing to speak one way or another. Let's say you ask your manager for her blessing for you to serve as the head of a new internal committee. She responds by telling you your workload is about to increase and therefore she doesn't want you to be saddled with distractions. Sitting quietly, you listen to her explanation, careful not to nod your head as though you're in agreement or jump in with a concession, but keeping an RNF. Again here, give yourself about seven seconds to be silent. This maneuver will often push your counterpart to explain their reasoning, sometimes even causing them to back out of it and come up with a different response altogether.

And hey, if silence is used on you, don't worry. You can handle a quiet period by making a point to look unfazed by the quiet. You can also ask deepening questions such as, "What are your thoughts on the proposal?" or "I'm curious, what you think about X?"

The next time you're in a negotiation situation, experiment with being quiet at moments that matter, rather than speaking up right away or thanking your counterpart. Although it can feel awkward at first, remember that silence gives you the gift of slack—and space for contemplation. There's no reason you can't have both.

 ## Don't Give Others Free Admission

One of my teenage jobs was working in a red, black, and white 1950s-style diner. I distinctly remember Liz, a tireless waitress, who carried two steaming coffee pots in one hand, and a tray of food and drinks in the other. Whoa, Liz, talk about being an overachiever!

For plenty of my career, I felt I should be the professional version of Liz. If someone added something to my load, I'd freely take it on and think to myself, *Okay, here comes a challenge—let's get on it!*

There I was trying to be excellent at everything. But one day—after a 70-hour workweek—I had a crushing realization: I didn't feel excellent at *anything!* I was doing so much that I didn't have the time or energy to give my all to anything. Can you relate? Have you ever taken on promise after commitment after extra work—all in the name of being a Liz-like, high-achieving team player?

The thing is, the most surefire way to burn out—to sink yourself—is to ignore your own limits and boundaries. Plus, it makes it really hard to perform remarkably when every task needs your best energy!

That's why I want to introduce you to two concepts you can apply to your interactions with others. They've helped me be more strategic about brokering outcomes with other people that meet their needs in a way that works for me too. Using these techniques, you can negotiate deadlines, yeses, and noes with more backbone and confidence!

- **Be selectively excellent:** Just like a successful business, you need to choose where you want to be particularly innovative or differentiated. Rather than trying to win at every project you touch, think about the one or two areas you really want to be defined by as a professional. Is it strategic thinking? Finance skills? Tech brilliance? Nonprofit management? Mentoring junior teammates? Taking those areas into account, how could you make exceptions to give more to those things and less to others? This way, you're lining up your discretionary effort with your distinct value. The more you identify these areas, aligning them with your time and energy investment, the more you can negotiate happier outcomes with people making demands on your time. This could sound like:

  - "I'd be totally willing to work on the ABC presentation and get it done by tonight, but can I look to someone else to help out with XYZ report?"

- **Limit choices, aka "The red shoes or gray shoes" technique:** The paradox of having loads of choices is that faced with too many selections, the average person experiences more anxiety and tends to feels worse. That's why rather than take an "always open" approach to accepting work or saying yes to people's demands, consider limiting the choices available to them. Think about it: if a kid is going out to play, we might say, "Do you want to wear your red shoes or your gray shoes?" Both shoes are suitable for playing and the kid gets to make the final choice. In a similar way, how can you start making a limited-option offering to someone making demands on your time? That way, if someone says to you, "I have an urgent situation I need your help with," you could say:

◆ "I'd be glad to find a way to help you out. I can either drop the X project and work on this urgent need or I could continue working on the X project and see if Lisa can help you."

Notice how you're not jumping to say a blanket "Yes" or offering an all-access pass to you until the end of time? By giving clear choices, you frame the possibilities and preferred approach. So what kind of choices are you going to make?

 ## Carry Yourself with a Sense of Purpose

Imagine this: you're the boss. Two people you manage are getting ready to make a big pitch to you for a new product idea. You're admittedly excited about the possibilities based on what you know.

This presentation is their chance to wow you, and you're looking forward to it!

The first person walks in looking self-assured. His shoulders are back and relaxed. He has an easy smile, makes engaged eye contact, and walks right up to you and starts chatting with you.

A few moments later, the second person walks in—late—having gotten diverted by side conversations on the way. Upon entering, he moves hurriedly to the corner of the room, where he's looking down, shuffling his papers haphazardly. He quickly looks up at you to nod "Hey," but his focus seems to be on preparing at the last minute!

Uh-oh, right? Just imagining this scenario, I bet you can feel in your body the difference between these two hypothetical presenters. It's visceral, isn't it?

The good news is when it comes to important negotiations and interactions, it's entirely possible to harness our bodies just like this first "presenter" did—to use them to support us and our message in a powerful way.

I'm talking about techniques you can use repeatedly to set a confident tone and feel your best. These practices, when you choose to use them, can send powerful signals to your brain to relax—freeing you up to do your best work! They also signal to those around you that you're ready and you're prepared with something to say.

- **Center before you enter:** Before you walk into a negotiation, protect at least five to ten minutes right beforehand to center yourself. This is a time to mentally transition out of what you were doing and into this moment now. You might be in a restroom for this, sitting in a cubicle, or in an office. Ideally you are in a relatively quiet space where you can tune into your intention for the conversation ahead—and get in a positive frame of mind.

- **Walk tall:** Straightening your posture so you stand and walk tall is one of those 10-second confidence boosts that never gets old! Stop right now and do this. Feel the difference when you put your shoulders back and really lengthen your body toward the sky. As you practice this step, walk like you have a clear destination in mind. That means you carry yourself like you're focused, you have a place to be!

- **Make an entrance:** From the minute you walk in the door to negotiate, you're setting a tone. Think carefully about what a self-assured, positive entrance looks like for you. For me, this means walking into the room using longer strides, maintaining eye contact, and having an easy smile from the first moment. It also means my personal items including folders, paper, or pens are relatively organized and ready to pull from.

These techniques, many of which set a tone early in the conversation, help you hit the ground running. And who doesn't like time savings? Remember, even getting 5% better at this each time you negotiate can add up over time. Start now, and get your next conversation off on the right foot.

 ## Negotiate with the Person, Not the Power

A young entrepreneur pulled me aside at a conference once and said, wide-eyed, "Can I ask you something? How do you get over the initial intimidation of working with these humongous companies?"

I understood her nerves and hesitation well. I think back to 28-year-old me negotiating my first large consulting contract with a Fortune 500 company. There I was by myself, brokering deal terms with their 30-person legal team. I felt totally intimidated.

But then something came into focus for me. I could continue to behave as though it was "little tiny me" versus a massive 30-person legal team. Or I could *stop negotiating with the power and start negotiating with the person* instead.

I decided then and there to negotiate with Melissa, the associate general counsel who was my main contact. She was a person (shocker!), not an establishment. And you know what? Making that shift pared down this scary negotiation into something way simpler: a conversation between two people, with the goal of agreement.

I'm a big believer this mindset can help you too. So how can you negotiate with the person, not the power?

- If you're outnumbered, for example in a high-pressure job interview panel, focus on making one connection, with one individual, at a time. That way you're not pressured to persuade the whole group seamlessly; you deal with one interaction and person separately.

- If you're daunted by the number of issues to solve in a negotiation, try writing them up on a whiteboard in front of your counterpart. Let's say you're trying to work through a set of issues with a peer at your company, on a project that effects both of you. You can cross each issue off, one at a time, as you go. This signals progress and sends a message that, together, you're able to overcome the issues in front of you.

- If you're at an important networking event with VIPs you want to meet and learn from, focus on building rapport with one or two individuals who you feel some natural chemistry or connection with. That ups the chances you'll develop a few memorable relationships and takes away the risk of engaging in several quick transactions.

- If you want to invite an executive at your company to have a career conversation with you but feel nervous or uncomfortable, remember they were not born an executive. They've learned, stumbled, and experienced trial and error along the way. Remembering that helps you see them as more than their impressive title alone.

There will be plenty of times in negotiations where we don't have the same exact amount of laurels as our counterpart. That's okay. The key is to make sure you're not assuming you're the weaker force as a default.

Expect some give-and-take as you bring your boldest ideas to life. But know you can always build purposeful relationships that honor your worth and stature. When you treat yourself with worthiness, you set the standard for how everyone else should be treated too.

 ## Defy Time Pressure

My coworker Maria once had a sign on her desk that read, "No pressure, no diamonds!"

We all want to feel like we can withstand tough pressure and come out better or stronger for it. But there's a kind of pressure at work that usually works against you— time pressure:

- It might be a job offer you only have one day to respond to (I affectionately call this "the exploding offer"). Ack!

- Maybe it's an agreement a vendor is pressuring you into signing to lock in a certain rate.
- Maybe it's a favor someone asks of you in the hallway or one-to-one in a Zoom chat, or an unexpected problem that requires you to stay late.

In these situations, especially if you're dealing with an authority figure, there can be a very real pressure to say yes or follow the other person's lead.

But guess what? Giving in to that pressure doesn't prioritize your time, confidence, or needs.

If you're uncomfortable or unsure about the terms in front of you, don't feel locked in. Instead, try these techniques the next time someone compels you to act fast:

1. **Don't answer then and there.** One of the most empowering practices in my life has been learning to delay my answers when I get "an exploding offer." Here's what I mean: next time you're faced with that drive-by request from someone in the hallway, create a window of space before you answer. Tell them, "I need to look at my calendar and get back to you before I can answer" or "Let me think about it and get back to you" or "I need to check with so-and-so first." That way you're not saying yes as a default or reflex. You give yourself time and space to assess the request and say yes as a 100% active choice.

2. **Renegotiate the window of time you're given.** Throughout your career, people will put their urgent issues on your shoulders. Do not, I repeat, do not try to be the rescuer of everyone else's emergency! When people offer you a short window of time—to consider a job offer, for example—get in the habit of negotiating

to elongate the window. You could say, "I'd be more comfortable with three days instead of one to consider this—can we make that work?" You never have to agree to a time limit just because it's given.

3. **Don't apologize for things you haven't done wrong.**
   If you can't deliver on someone's request, you might wanna say sorry. But just like hot fudge sundaes (my favorite!), too much apologizing can be bad for us. Instead of sending the message that you're lacking, consider saying, "I checked my schedule, and I won't be able to help out this time." Realize that apologizing is a great practice for correcting wrongs, but don't do it when someone else's need doesn't line up with your realities—that's not your fault, that's just life!

As a professional, you face pressure from lots of different angles—but *you are in charge* of what you agree to. Your own self-confidence and self-respect are too important to put behind someone else's needs or inconsideration.

So negotiate for your time and stand up to the pressure—future you depends on it!

 ## When It Comes to Money, Don't Laugh

"Don't turn them off by looking greedy!"

"Take what you're given."

"Why don't you just accept the offer before they change their mind?"

I'm not going to lie. I was horrified when my friend told me she got a new job offer and her mom gave her this negotiating advice!

If you've ever worried that stating an ambitious compensation figure would kill your chances of getting a job or winning a piece of business, you are not alone. But let me tell you, this habit isn't doing you any favors! Adam D. Galinsky, a professor at Columbia Business School, researched this phenomenon and found that most negotiators make wimpy first offers.[6] That's usually driven by factors such as our confidence and perceived level of control at the bargaining table.

Galinsky's work showed that many negotiators fear making an aggressive first offer will alarm or annoy the other side and maybe even cause them to walk away, but this fear is usually exaggerated. Realize that whenever you start with an ambitious opening number, you drive the rest of the deal in your favor more than you realize.

To challenge this "accept less" belief, it's important to make a point to "round up" instead of "rounding down." Here are two important ways to do that:

- **Lean on what you can justify:** Your opening number should be the most aggressive figure *you can rationally defend!* That means bringing a set of data, research, benchmarks (or another job offer) you can point to as evidence for your strong opening number. This might sound like: "Based on my research of senior project manager compensation in our market, I'm looking to be in the neighborhood of $180,000" or "Given I have another offer for $180,000, I'd be open to continuing the interview process if you can match that salary."

- **Make it the highest number you can say without LOLing (laughing out loud):** Here's one way to know you're making an aggressive offer: if you were to get

it, it would thrill and delight you. Notice I'm not saying it would satisfy you or merely "cover your bases."
Rounding up in this way often requires thinking of
yourself differently—as more senior, more experienced,
or more valuable than you're typically accustomed.
This usually sounds assertive, short and sweet—as in:
"I'd like to be at the $180,000 mark" or "I'm open to
exploring new opportunities for roles in the vicinity of
$180,000."

Still skeptical? Consider this: experiments conducted by
University of Idaho professor Todd J. Thorsteinson[7] showed
that study participants were more likely to offer a subject
$5,000 more in salary if she asked for an implausibly high
salary—compared to asking for a lower salary.

Wowza! Bravery *literally pays*.

Remember, by coming to the bargaining table at all, a
person is usually willing to negotiate something! Bring your
most creative mindset, and don't be afraid to invent new
solutions that make all parties feel like they're coming out
ahead. Your ambitious starting number opens the door to
all kinds of exciting possibilities.

 ## Defang "No"

Remember when I told you I was invited to interview to
be a global spokesperson for a tech company? And how the
interview came, went—and bombed? I was wracked with
feeling like I wasn't good enough for the opportunity. I
acted like I didn't belong, watered down my "me-ness," and
definitely didn't bring my best.

I can still remember the brevity of the rejection email I received afterward: "Thanks for coming to meet with us, Selena. We're going to pass—but stay in touch."

Well, a week later, after mourning this missed opportunity with my head under my down blanket, I decided to take them at their word. I had nothing to lose by keeping in touch, like they suggested.

I wrote to them and proposed a fresh idea: that we codesign a study on professionals' negotiation habits—timing the results with the launch of my book *Pushback*. And they liked the idea. In fact, they agreed! The result of the partnership was a worldwide survey, which generated some eye-opening findings. The company engaged a major PR firm and made me the spokesperson of the study. Over several weeks, I was thrilled to represent our work in front of major media such as the *LA Times*, MSNBC, CNN, TodayShow.com, and many others.

Talk about an unexpected ending!

The point is, "No" is not always the end of the story. As you hear your share of noes, keep these mindset shifts in mind:

- **Be Tenacious.** When we act tenaciously in spite of a no, it communicates to us and others that we're determined. Think about it: if you get a job rejection, and you're quick to abandon the position that you were a fitting candidate, you have to wonder how much you wanted the job in the first place! That's why I want you to start embracing the quality of tenacity. See it as a badge of honor, a symbol of your grit and self-belief. Madeline Y. Bee, a STEM professional, did this when she applied for the same scholarship for three years in a row—until she received it. As Madeline puts it, "There's something to be said for being persistent. Persistence shows commitment, passion, and an ability to get things done . . . [it's] also an exercise in practicing." Inspiring, right? As you build your own tenacity, think about how you can use an initial loss or rejection as a "practice run" to set you up differently the next time.

- **Show You Believe in Yourself.** When you're handed a rejection, don't confirm their opinion that you're the wrong fit. If anything, show your unshakeable self-belief! Sarah Eadie, a marketing professional in Texas, did this. After being rejected from her top-choice company following a first-round interview, Sarah stayed positive and continued to build rapport with the recruiter. That same recruiter said she might be able to get Sarah a networking coffee meeting with the hiring manager even if she wasn't offered an onsite interview. That coffee meeting happened and rather than press for the job she didn't get, Sarah focused on future possibilities. After that meeting, the hiring manager asked Sarah if she'd be open to a position with the company. In the end, the company adjusted the open position to accommodate Sarah. And with the help of her coach, Jamie Lee, Sarah successfully negotiated a job offer that resulted in a $15K salary increase.

It's not a question of *if* you'll hear "No" in your career, it's *when*. Remembering that rejection is common—and often surmountable—is what'll help you be ready to pivot. Where will you try to flip a "No" to a "Yes"? Now's the perfect time to start!

6 Harness High-Stakes Moments

A journalist once asked me my best advice for anyone getting ready to give a TED talk.

I said that preparing will feel *like a three-month-long fever dream.*

Ha! That might sound like an exaggeration, but I wasn't kidding.

Delivering my TEDx talk felt like the Empire State building of high-stakes moments for me. Going after this goal meant I could put an amplifier to ideas that could help people being marginalized at work and make a difference. And given the video format, it meant I'd be seen and heard.

At the time, I was bursting with determination to share my practical ideas for stopping gender bias at work. I applied to six or seven events around the world, and following a series of auditions, I was invited to speak at TEDxHartford.

Can you say #lifegoals?! What a high and an honor to be part of this world.

But the talk was intimidating, I won't lie. It was without a doubt one of those "put on your big girl pants" moments.

As the big day got closer, it turned out all of the days, weeks, and months of flipping through my floppy, dog-eared set of index cards on a metal ring paid off. There I stood, on a red dot, on the most beautiful stage I'd ever seen—in my fiercest blue dress—ready to give an 18-minute presentation by memory.

And I did it.

The talk was a success and, for me, it was a pivotal point that taught me the power of grabbing hold of a high-stakes opportunity and turning it into a real growth moment. While I don't have the craving to do it again, I can say that rising to this particular high-stakes moment is up there—no, at the top—of my list of life experiences.

If only I knew the momentum wasn't done yet!

Imagine my surprised-freaking-joy when a few months later, I got a notice that I had won the Croly Journalism award for the reporting I did in my TEDx talk. Along with this exciting honor came a cash prize and opportunity to receive the award and give a speech in Austin, Texas.

I flew to Austin with my amazing husband, Geoff, and did my best to give a speech to 1,000+ people that would stir something inside them, that would make them want to amplify the voices of the girls and women in their lives.

After I was done, I received a standing ovation.

Just. Whoa.

It wasn't lost on me that if I hadn't applied to those original TEDx talks, not a single one of those other transformative experiences would have happened to me. How cool is it that one brave action can create a chain reaction?!

Now if this version of the story sounds like a runaway train of good luck and opportune moments, you're not off in your interpretation.

But what I haven't shared yet are the many people I needed to enlist to be part of this journey with me. The coach I hired to help me walk through my talking points, the editor I hired to reread my speech, the (constant) pep talks from my family and best friends that I wasn't absurd to think I could do this.

Another thing you didn't hear about yet was the trade-off I needed to make so that TEDx could fit into my life. I couldn't always go to dinners out or a movie with my family because I had to practice my speech and I had to be honest about those trade-offs. Like it or not, that was just part of the deal. The fact is, when we go after something BIG, there *are* costs! We might need to carve out more time for our aspiration, which takes away time from other important things or people. Or, no matter how disciplined we might be, even when we're off the clock, we might find it hard not to give our thinking and mental energy to our cause.

There's also the possibility that when you want to go after a high-stakes opportunity, like asking for venture capital for your business or giving a talk or asking for a promotion, you may feel some real angst and neuroticism leading up to it. It might be hard to relax when your body and mind are getting the message, in neon flashing lights, that something BIG is on the line.

I don't tell you this to dissuade you in any way from your high-stakes moment. Sometimes these perceived *threats* are actually the opportunity of a lifetime!

In fact, it's no wonder neuroscience tells us we go into fight, flight, or freeze mode when we face a high-stakes or threatening situation. Oftentimes, we perceive high-stakes situations *as threats* because we feel like these moments will make or break our careers.

As you work on your everyday confidence, I want to help you recognize the especially meaningful, high-stakes moments in your career. I developed the tips in this chapter to help manage my anxiety before these kinds of events, and I know you can benefit from them too.

Look, the more you raise your hand with a "Hell yes!" to those opportunities that "exhilify" you (both exhilarate and terrify you), the more you will start to believe you earned your spot. And you can and will reliably follow through. Each time you bet on yourself in these moments, you show yourself what you're capable of.

So instead of waiting until you "feel ready"—for one more year of experience on the job or one more degree, or one more fill-in-the-blank—I'm here to ask you *to do it afraid.*

After all, security is kind of an illusion anyway. We might think we're playing it safe by sitting on the sidelines but that hardly makes us untouchable.

Imagine walking through life quietly knowing you can do scary, hard things. And what if you had a slate of real experiences you could look to, as proof you've stood at the edge of your comfort zone time and again, and survived? Grown even!

When you take these techniques and make them your own, you will find yourself in squishy, new, and different situations. But guess what? You can manage it with humility, self-respect, and a learning mindset. As you rise to new heights, may you be guided by my favorite question of all time: *What would you do if you weren't afraid?*

Managing the Relationship with Your Boss

One of my all-time favorite coffee mugs reads, "I never asked . . . to be the World's Best Boss." Ha! In seriousness though, the relationship with your boss is a special one—it's high stakes! And it deserves special treatment.

Whether your bond with your boss is brand-new or years old, one special element of this relationship is that it's interdependent: your boss needs you for your contributions. And most likely you depend on them too—for direction and to be an advocate.

If you want to build your confidence in this relationship, you can do it, no matter what your starting point. In fact, I bet your bond can be even more productive, engaging, and cooperative. Use these three strategies to make meaningful connections with your boss right away:

- **Observe their preferences.** One of the most important things in communication is hearing what isn't said. Notice the cues your boss gives you: sighs of exasperation, smiles of happiness, their slumped or alert posture. When you notice your boss's body language, you can take those cues to speed up your pace—for example, to be more enthusiastic, or to address a potential concern. When listening, loosen up your torso so you can lean in with interest at a particularly powerful point, or on the flip side, sit back in your chair and take in the broad view of what's being said. You can alternate nodding as you listen to your boss's points and gesturing to emphasize your own points. Paying attention to their engagement helps you bring your full energy to these interactions.

- **Remember bosses are people too!** To build confidence in your bond, remember that demonstrating basic caring and kindness can go a long way with your manager. After all, they most likely wear several hats in their life beside "boss." So remember to ask them "How are you?" or "Did you enjoy the holiday?" By not being all-business, you're more likely to spark a friendly connection. Mind you, you're not aiming to be best friends here, which can get really complicated. This is about humanizing the relationship, and sharing some of those positive, more personal moments together.

- **Be reliable (not just when it's convenient).** Reliability is essential in most relationships—and it's critical with your boss. Strive to be dependable in your everyday actions. For example, if you say you'll have your timesheet in by Friday, do it. On the flip side, if you're tempted to say, "I'll write up a recap of what we discussed today," don't make an offer like that if you're not going to do it. If your manager has to second-guess the commitments you make, even little ones, it hurts your reputation and your bond. Remember, if you want to be trusted, you have to be trustworthy.

At the end of the day, your boss is your number one customer—your VIP at your organization. By taking these steps you can show them you're consistently reliable and resourceful, which will only build your confidence—and encourage mutual trust and respect. Remember, you need each other.

Assume Everyone's Awkward

Shortly after the COVID-19 pandemic quarantine lifted, I was invited to a special social gathering, and almost immediately my head started to spin. Part of me was jumping at excitement to get out and do something social and fun. The other part of me was wondering if I'd ever remember how to make words come out of my mouth with actual people! If I knew how to "human" anymore.

Have you felt similarly at times?

Then this is a great time to make a few things really clear. If you have more social anxiety than usual, especially after a big life change (such as a pandemic, losing a loved one, moving, or having a baby), you are not alone. If socializing makes you feel ambivalent right now, that is normal. And if you feel rusty at socializing, that's perfectly okay.

The beauty here is that it's possible to overcome that awkwardness in high-stakes moments and find some inner solace. That way, you can walk into new rooms and situations and interact with ease—and without undue pressure or a need to get it "perfect."

Here are some tips you can use right away:

- **Believe EVERYONE is awkward.** Or at the very least, I want you to acknowledge we all have the capacity to be bizarre, uncool, and socially inept at times. Think about it: at a given party, someone is putting their foot in the mouth, someone else is drawing attention to something their friend doesn't appreciate, while another person is telling a story that borders on oversharing.

The point is, you're not the only one who's not a natural at socializing all the time. Realize everyone is doing their best—and no one is there to assess your particular level of awkwardness and then revel in your defects.

- **"One size" fits none.** There's no one way to socialize or build rapport. Truly, there is no "right and wrong" socializing rulebook. So rather than falling prey to the "spotlight effect," where you believe all eyes are intently watching and monitoring you, reassure yourself that even in a high-stakes moment, people don't know what you're experiencing. Then use that moment as an opportunity to pivot from focusing on yourself to focusing on someone you're socializing with—for example, by asking them a question.

- **After a high-stakes moment or gathering, don't do a lengthy post-mortem.** If things don't go exactly as you hoped, resist the urge to replay in your mind's eye every single encounter "to review it for awkwardness or cringe-worthy moments." Some moments will be smooth and some certainly won't, but the way you're going to build up self-trust and confidence is to experience an event—and then let it go. It's not very helpful to litigate every awkward word, look, or moment—so lightly brush off your meeting or event and leave it behind you. When it comes to your life, you always have the final word!

The great thing about awkwardness is that it never killed anyone. It's an extension of being human. And it's often proof we're trying to connect with others (even if it doesn't go seamlessly). Giving yourself and others permission to be a little awkward is hugely liberating. Immediately you'll feel some weight lift. And you might just surprise yourself as the grounded, self-assured leader who makes a point to include and welcome all types.

Visualize Yourself in the Act

Writing my first book, *The Next Generation of Women Leaders,* was an unbelievable proposition. Obviously, there was the fact that I had never done it before. But there was also this issue: I couldn't even picture this dream I had coming true! That is, until one day when I decided I needed to "see it to believe it."

So, with the help of my friend Melissa, I made a fake book cover and wrapped it around an old manual I had lying around. I added the cover image I imagined on the front of the book—showing a powerful woman leader. I included "By Selena Rezvani" in prominent letters, and I even added a few accolades on the front cover from newspapers. This "picture" is what helped me finish that book! It moved the concept of writing a book from a hypothetical to a high-stakes reality.

For most people, it helps to first picture yourself, in your current body, attaining your goals. The practice of visualization means simply forming a mental image in your mind. It can be as simple as a single mental picture or it can play in your mind like a scene in a movie. And it's a strategy lots of top professional athletes rely on. In fact, for Simone Biles, the most decorated American gymnast alive, she credits visualizing goals—like making the national team—and building her self-belief as keys to her success.

And you know what? It's no different for you.

Visualization helps us feel like we're physically there—in a powerful place we hope to be. That's because when people picture a goal in advance of actually doing it, the same regions of the brain are stimulated as when we perform it in real life. So imagine for a minute preparing to deliver a critical presentation. As you prepare your remarks, you build a visualization of yourself: standing in front of a screen, speaking knowledgeably, appearing engaged but relaxed. Doing this visualization tricks your brain into thinking you've already done something similar and succeeded, which boosts your motivation and performance.

The best thing about doing this is you can construct a positive, personalized visualization of your own. Not just for a project you're working on right now, but in a repeatable way, at any time in your life. Let's walk through some steps to practice visualizing your future goal:

1. **See success.** Choose a high-stakes moment where you really want to do well. Now start to imagine an outstanding result in this part of your life—whatever that would look like for you. Really see the best possible outcome. What does it look like? What specifically are you doing? What are you wearing? And what's happening around you? How are people reacting to you? Work here to ignore roadblocks or negative thoughts—try to focus on seeing the best outcome.

2. **Activate your senses.** Now go a little deeper. Try to make this picture even more vivid and detailed by using your senses. What does your voice sound like? What are your hands touching or holding? What's the taste in your mouth? What are you looking at it and seeing? Make sure this image feels gratifying and positive. Mentally take a snapshot of this image so you can easily recall it. Then picture shrinking it down to the size of a coin. Imagine putting it in your pocket, where you can grab it and *become it* any time.

3. **Put your struggle with this goal in the past.** Close your eyes and conjure up one more picture. To really cement the idea that you can grow and overcome

struggles, think of someone you trust. After identifying them, visualize having a conversation with them where you talk about your struggle or the story of your growth in past tense. The "you" in this visualization might look like the present-day you or it could look like an older, wiser you from the future. Either way, practice talking about your critical learning as something that's been achieved, that you worked through. Doing this builds your sense of optimism that you can advance yourself and it will help you detach, in a healthy way, from problems that may have dogged you in the past.

Great job—you did it! Whenever you need to sharpen your focus and confidence, repeat this visualization. By rehearsing your future success, you'll internalize your pictures so that they become real actions. As you do, don't forget to add smells, littles details, and imagery to really bring it to life. Then share that learning with someone else. Remember, "You've got to see it to be it." So create a compelling picture—one that future you can't wait to live up to.

 ## Keys to Thinking on Your Feet

Do you ever freeze under pressure? Or panic when you're called on in a meeting?

Hey, that's understandable!

Most of us like to be prepared for tough questions, at least a little bit.

The great news is this is learnable—you *can* answer even the most difficult questions with poise, even when you haven't specifically prepared for them. That way, you'll exude confidence, even when you're improvising.

Here are five ways to speak with self-assurance when you're put on the spot:

1. **First, pause and breathe.** Take a good, solid inhalation before you speak. This does two things: It gives you a brief pause so you can gather your thoughts and get your footing. And it does something else: it boosts the supply of oxygen to your brain, which quiets your mind and promotes calm feelings. The less familiar you are with the nature of the question, the slower you should go in answering.

2. **Next, organize your thoughts.** One of the simplest ways to deliver a coherent answer to a hard question is to use a simple framework such as *What–So What–Now What* or even *Past-Present-Future*. That means that rather than deliver a stream-of-consciousness or jumbled answer, you give a reliable, articulate one.

   a. With *What–So What–Now What* you start with explaining the "What." What matters? What essential facts, observations, or patterns stand out? Then ask yourself, "So what? Why is that important? What are the implications? Finally, frame your response in terms of the future by asking yourself, "Now what?" What actions make sense going forward? Based on what I know, what do I recommend as next steps?

   b. With *Past-Present-Future*, you can answer on the spot by starting to share a relevant piece of context from the past. As in, what was the lead-up to the situation today? Then, address the present by answering the question "What's most relevant right now?" Lastly, address the future with even one or two sentences. You can answer the question "What can we expect as a next step or immediate development?"

3. **Buy yourself more time.** If you're truly in unknown territory, you can negotiate to extend the timeline that you provide information or give an answer. Here's the thing though—you can't always do this. Buy yourself more time to answer questions no more than 15% of the time. That means in the remaining time you give strong opinions and answers based primarily on trusting *what you do know*.

If you put these practices to work and you still find you've rambled off course, not to worry. Summarize your main position in one sentence, stated strongly and firmly at the end.

The next time you need to come up with something dazzling on your feet, reach for these tools. Others will notice your confidence and ideas. You'll position yourself as someone who's in control, with a thoughtful approach—and great reflexes.

 ## Create a Memory Palace

Picture this: you're in a big deal meeting, and everyone is looking at you expectantly, depending on you to say a precise message.

That's when it happens: your mind goes completely blank. Kaput! Slate wiped clean.

Horrifying, right?

If you can feel your heart rate elevating just *imagining* such a scenario, you're not alone! It's a nail-biting situation for most of us.

But whether your high-stakes moment is public speaking, a pitch, or a one-on-one meeting, you can use a "memory palace" to recollect your key points. This mnemonic technique, created in ancient times, works because it helps make associations between new information and old information you already know.

This technique requires choosing a place you know well, like your home or a favorite park. Then, mentally picture walking through that place, assigning your key points to certain landmarks to make it more memorable.

So, if you're preparing to talk about a new product idea, for example, and you want to commit your flow and messages to memory, overlay your three-part message onto the picture of your home and then do as follows:

1. Talk about the main product idea as you imagine opening the front door and entering the hallway.
2. Picture turning left into your living room, which marks when you'll discuss the monetization of the product.
3. Then make another left into your kitchen as you discuss the marketing of the product.

See how it works? It's even more effective if you can add some sensory or colorful detail—like feeling your bare feet sink into a thick rug as you walk across it. Or glancing at a funny magnet on your fridge as you round the corner in your kitchen.

I know at first this can be counterintuitive. It feels like it's actually *more work*, because you need to conjure up twice the reference material! But I promise it works and can even give you a little bonus—a sense of comfort in terms of "being" in a familiar place. I used my own home to help me memorize my TEDx talk and actually walking the rooms while I practiced my lines really helped my message stick in my mind.

I recommend walking through your journey several times with your eyes closed as you speak to your points, graduating to doing it with your eyes open. Then you'll be ready to remember your main messages at the moment it matters most, without the danger of blanking!

Get Good at Gesturing

When you're trying to convince an audience to see things your way, do you purposely check your body language to see if it matches your message?

Most people I talk to say an emphatic "No!" when I ask this question.

So why does it even matter?

When we're making an appeal to others, it helps to use our bodies to reinforce our message. Research shows gesturing is not so much an add-on or extra to what you're saying verbally, it's an essential part of the central meaning people are taking away. In one study in *Cognitive Research: Principles and Implications,*[1] researchers found that seeing gestures that represented actions enhanced understanding. Even more interesting, gestures tend to map to different meanings even more directly than language does!

Add to this that those who gesture more often while speaking are seen as more engaging to listen to—and warmer—than those who minimally gesture. Going back to making positive first impressions, we know that warmth is an important quality to display early on, even before confidence.

My best of rule of thumb to embrace gesturing is to use finger, hand, and arm movements that align with your words.

So, for example, if you're counting out a list of issues, you can use your index, middle, and ring fingers to physically count out the items. The following is a reference list for some other common gestures. Note this is not an exhaustive list, nor are these suggestions the only suitable way to gesture. Use them as a starting point and make them your own:

Message	Gesture	Message	Gesture
Shrink costs	Pinch your index finger and thumb together until touching	You	With palm open, slide your hand horizontally
Three levels	Chop the air with your hand three times, progressing vertically	Welcome!	Arm stretch in front of torso with palms open
Me/I	Point to your chest	Expanding our customer base	Expand your arms outwardly
Come together	Bring your open palms together to touch	A tiny bit	Pinch your index finger and thumb together
This needs to stop	Raise your hand in front of your torso, with palm facing away from you	A spike or growth in sales	Make a checkmark in the air with your index finger

See how these little movements "put a bow" on your words and strengthen your message? Using your body in this way helps you come across as more engaging, persuasive, and credible. Don't leave it out of your repertoire when you need to capture people's attention!

Secrets from Media Training

I'll never forget some years ago watching actress Anne Hathaway skillfully handle a media interview. She was on an international tour to promote her new film, *Les Mis*. Yet from the start of one particular Q&A, the host kept bringing the conversation back to Anne's recent (and embarrassing) wardrobe malfunction. Yikes! But not only did Anne control the interview with finesse, steering away from the interviewer's topic of conversation, she was widely praised after the fact for how she handled the interview.

While you may or may not find yourself being interviewed on national television, we can all learn from Anne. See, Anne *expected* curveball questions—*she anticipated them*—and clearly prepared. The great thing here is you can too. Being ready for challenging conversations and tough questions—whether in job interviews or high-stakes meetings—matters. Not only do your answers in these moments cement your reputation as a leader, they also forge your own self-confidence in a powerful way.

Here are the secrets I've learned from going through media training and acting as a spokesperson more than once. Use these tips to power-up your communication:

1. **Never repeat a negative premise or question.** Just because someone asks you a question, does not mean

you need to approve or authorize it. That's why if someone says to you, "Is it true you have doubts about the
new leadership?" you should not repeat the negative
framing. First of all, this question may be taking you far
off track from the message you actually want to share.
Second, by repeating back a negative statement, you can
be quoted as saying something you don't mean! Instead,
you choose the framing. For example, you could say,
"Here's how I actually view leadership and [add more
detail]" or "I don't agree with that stance. Here's what I
think . . ."

2. **You can steer *any conversation*.** When you're asked a
   tough or diminishing question, commit to the belief
   that you can actively guide that conversation in a direction that respects your boundaries. No one is owed or
   entitled to information; it's up to you to decide what is
   shared and how. After you accept this fact, make friends
   with the concept of bridging. This means instead of
   answering a trivial, negative, or disrespectful question,
   you pivot—and instead make a bridge to what you do
   want to share. For example, if someone is pushing for
   your take on a silly rumor, you could say, "Here's the
   real issue in front of us . . ." or "What matters most in
   this situation is X . . ." or "Actually in this context, I
   should note X . . ." This guides the conversation to the
   more meaningful issue at hand.

3. **Don't speak for others.** Across your career, you may be
   asked to weigh in about someone else's situation, but
   I encourage you to find the confidence *not to take the
   bait*. Not only can you inadvertently erase or diminish
   the actual experience of the person you're speculating

about, you can easily get in trouble if your comments are taken out of context. So if someone says to you, "You must be shocked by your competitor's collapse," respond with "I'll let X comment on their own behalf, but what we're focused on right now is Y." The lesson is simple here: let the source speak for themselves.

Never underestimate the fact that *you* shape and mold what's up for discussion. Speak as a leader. Speak so people listen.

Don't Squirm from the Spotlight

Have you ever hungered for more recognition—but then squirmed when a colleague talked you up? Or maybe you were excited about taking on a visible career opportunity—only to feel weird with "all eyes on you"? This push and pull between both craving attention—and let's be honest—hating it is not uncommon.

Some people fear that reaching a new level means they have to keep *outdoing* their personal best. Others worry that with increased attention from others, every little action they take will be under a microscope. Still others think wanting some attention in the first place is selfish or petty.

Well, let's get some things straight. To want some attention, recognition, or notice is not wrong or bad. (I don't mean constantly being the center of attention in situations, mind you.) It can be very healthy to test what you can do by making your work seen, having a clear voice, and making an impact with larger audiences and communities than you're used to.

So what can you do if you're plagued by regret after putting "yourself out there" or going big? Try these simple steps
for confidently regaining your footing:

- **Anticipate your bodily alarms:** I remember in my
  favorite college humanities class, raising my hand with
  an important point I wanted to make. I felt eager to
  share it, making enthusiastic eye contact with the professor to call on me—only to feel my heart beat out of
  my chest the moment she did. Have you been there?
  When we put ourselves out there, we need to *expect*
  that we will indeed get that jolt of physical fear somewhere along the way. It is not a failure or a bug to be
  corrected; that fear is part of the very cycle of growth
  and progress. So expect that whenever you level-up and
  gain new forms of attention, your fear will be activated.
  Acknowledge and expect it, but don't inhabit it.

- **Tell your body it's not in danger, it's vulnerable:**
  Feeling a little more susceptible to others' opinions or
  reactions happens when we stretch what we can do.
  Here's the thing: vulnerability is a prerequisite of courage. As Brené Brown says, "The foundational skill set
  of courage-building is 'rumbling with vulnerability.'"
  Realize that if you are going to lead, teach others, or
  make an impact, you need to bring your humanity—
  your vulnerable parts. So, as you make bold moves
  that put you further into the spotlight, lean in to your
  vulnerabilities instead of shying away from them.
  Notice how your vulnerability makes your body feel
  different. Then use that. Your voice might quake when
  you say something moving. Or maybe you had a major
  learning moment you can share with others—that took
  you from a dejected place to a better place. Bring that

emotion . . . let your body tremble! Doing this will not only help you own and communicate your own narrative, it'll build trust and openness with others too.

- **Program a new channel:** The awkwardness of being seen for who we really are, warts and all, makes it easy to want to hide or flush with embarrassment. After all, our bodies are taking signals from our brains all the time about how to show up or be present. So rather than compounding a feeling of shame or embarrassment with messages of "I better hide" or "I better get out of here," tell your body the opposite. "I'm absolutely fine as I am." "I'm perfectly imperfect." Or "I love getting to show up authentically as me." The beauty is, it works. And it allows you and your body to realize life does not depend on this one situation going well.

It's perfectly normal to have moments when you both crave and hate attention. By training your body to welcome and use the fearful parts, you can show up as the best version of you in high-stakes moments. Use your body language to show you're authentic, you're enough, and you're ready.

 ## Confidently Speak to VIPs

When I had the chance to meet one of my heroes in leadership and management, I felt like my son's toy lightning ball. On the inside, I was pulsating with electricity, nerves, and excitement (heavy on the nerves!). Has that ever happened to you?

It's completely natural to feel nervous about meeting someone important in your industry. Chances are, you're feeling nervous because you admire them and want to impress them—this is a good thing! You can use that energy to prepare, stay aware, and keep yourself on point.

But let's be real, your nervous energy can also be your enemy. If we don't learn how to control it, it can prevent us from taking action and showing off the best parts of ourselves.

Meeting important people is an incredible opportunity to network, insert yourself into the professional circles you covet, and learn from others who have *mastered* the skills you're still refining. Realistically, you can catapult your career by light-years just by striking up a conversation with a VIP and drawing a common thread between you both!

People always ask me for advice on how to talk to important people in and outside of work. Just like anyone else, sometimes, I'm still filled with butterflies on the inside!

But I've figured out how to channel that buzz of energy, make a good impression, and say exactly what I want to say.

Here's how you can do it, too.

- **Put yourself in the path of more opportunities with VIPs.** Right now, I want you to look for at least two opportunities to get more exposure to executives in the next month. Maybe this is a one-to-one interview, a casual career conversation over lunch, or a panel discussion you attend where a VIP is speaking. Maybe it involves following a VIP on social media and commenting on their posts. By gaining more exposure and interaction with these individuals, you will lessen the sense you're an outsider or have nothing to say. When you up the frequency of your interactions with VIPs, it tells your brain "I regularly converse and interact with VIPs" and ultimately "I can do it in an assured and relaxed way."

- **Stay in the moment.** Sometimes, when we're most tense and worried, our minds get the message they should jump ahead and troubleshoot future scenarios. Ack! That can cause us to mentally make an exit, nodding and going through the motions in the very moment we want to be fresh and present. So, rather than letting your mind wander, give yourself license to focus on one. Thing. At a time. The message being imparted, the volley of ideas, whatever it may be. This is a lot easier when you accept things as they are. So tell yourself, "I am here now. By being present, I'm creating, shaping, and influencing what happens next."

In addition to speaking to VIPs peer to peer, like we explored in Chapter 3, put these tips to use next time you're meeting with a bigwig. If you stay calm with them, you can stay calm with anyone!

7 Overcome Toxic People and Cultures

Some people just ooze toxicity. They can bring down even the most positive, upbeat people around them. That's not just anecdotal. Research shows that negative colleagues can decrease other people's job performance and even their commitment to the organization.[1]

I know this dynamic well because . . . I was one of those toxic people.

Ugh, right? It hurts to admit it, but it's true. Let me tell you the story.

When I was 24, faced with the painful reality that I didn't like my career in social work, I knew I needed to pivot my skills elsewhere and try something new. Now, I have the *utmost* respect for social workers. They dedicate themselves to helping and equipping some of the most vulnerable people, but I myself simply could not hack it. After counseling violent crime victims, HIV-positive individuals, and domestic violence survivors, I had lost more than ten pounds, couldn't turn off any of my work thoughts on the weekend, and felt chronically anxious. I was disappointed in myself that I couldn't manage and, frankly, pretty ashamed.

Well, imagine my relief when I found a role at a nearby consulting firm whose clients were nonprofit organizations. It felt like the perfect bridge opportunity to bring my problem-solving skills from social work and apply them to nonprofit clients who wanted to have a bigger impact. While the role was about two levels too junior for my skills, I applied for the position, was offered it, and accepted.

Pretty early on, I saw that my relationship with my boss was not going to be a close or collegial one. She barked commands at me, had disappointment in her voice at all times, was gruff and even mean. I'll never forget noticing how other coworkers, including her coleaders, moved out of the way when they heard her name. They would raise their eyebrows up as if to tell me, "You better not screw this up . . . good luck with that!"

See, my boss had been through many coordinators and assistants over the years. What made our relationship even more transactional was that we interacted only over the phone, since she very rarely came into the office. That further drained any humanity that there might've been in our relationship.

Thank goodness there was another woman my age, Andrea, who understood the situation and was sympathetic! We ate lunch together, even socialized on weekends, and provided much needed comic relief for each other. Andrea felt like a godsend.

But, as the months passed, the grating comments from my boss increased. She saw no need to say hello before launching into a long list of orders. She'd yell, for example, about sections of a report that were missing but we'd never discussed. She presumed that things would automatically go wrong—as though I were helplessly incompetent.

And you know what? Slowly, I started to buy into that way of thinking, too. I soaked in the toxic feeling of my job like a second skin. It was part of me in social outings, on my lunch break, at my desk at the office—even at home, with my now-husband. That's the thing about toxic jobs. So often, when you're employed in one, so is your spouse or immediately family—whether they like it or not.

As the months wore on, I vented to my friend Andrea constantly. After all, I *hated* the way I was treated. I hated how I felt too: resigned and trapped. Then one day, over lunch, Andrea told me with a reluctant, heavy look, "All your complaining is actually making things harder for me."

Whoa. It was like a stinging slap in the face. And you know what? *I needed to hear that.* Somehow, despite hating the negative environment I was working in, despite prizing myself as a generally positive person, I was creating a new level of negativity for someone else! I realized this was not okay and not how I wanted to be. It was not sustainable. My boss was a fixture at this consulting firm, had lots of cache, and wasn't going anywhere. That meant I needed to remove myself.

I wish I could tell you that working for 18 months at this place didn't leave its stain on me, but it did. For so many people, when you work in a toxic job, you internalize aspects of the bad treatment. You might think, *I really am incapable of getting anything right* (one of my boss's favorite blasts) or *Why can't you just fit in at this place and make this work?* Well, the residue from these jobs is real. Even today as a I write this, I have a deeply uncomfortable, visceral, physical reaction remembering the awful experience.

Yes, avoiding these environments in the first place is ideal, but no one enters them on purpose (I don't think). So let's acknowledge that if you get stuck in such an environment, it's not your fault and you really do need to take some time to heal. And as much as we've progressed as a society raising issues such as burnout, mental health, and problematic toxic work cultures (even our surgeon general has raised this issue), many people don't know what to do when it's *actually happening* to them.

Well, I'm here to tell you there are ways out.

The thing is, even if your self-esteem has taken a hit, it starts with *believing* you can do better. And *you deserve better!* Don't wait for a signed letter from the universe—act on your own behalf. That might sound laughably simple, but it's profoundly true. The tips in this chapter are meant to help you with exactly that belief. As you consider ways to protect your peace—physically, mentally, and interpersonally— I promise you can become stronger at this, regardless of your starting point.

The best part is that you'll start to recognize when you yourself are showing up in not-so-great ways, too. And you'll get a much better radar for when other people are being toxic as well. That boosts your self-confidence and ability to make choices that line up with your values.

The techniques that follow are all about keeping your dignity and your self-respect as you move out of harmful situations. So whether you're trying to cope with other people's frantic energy, you need a comeback for noxious gossiping or backstabbing, or you're trying to survive morale-crushing favoritism, I'm here for you, and I know you can get through this.

You may not be able to prevent toxic people from coming around. But you can most certainly prevent them from staying.

Remember you have this *one life*. Anything that costs you your peace is too expensive!

Stress Is Contagious and You Can Avoid Catching It

Imagine you're sitting there, doing your work—or having an ordinary conversation—when an authority figure thunders angrily into the room. *Yikes,* right? Talk about a change in the atmosphere. I bet you can feel it from where you're reading this! You know from experience how quickly the mood of a place can transform. Stress is a lot like that—when one individual feels it strongly, it's like a baton that gets passed around from person to person to person.

Science supports this idea.

In one study,[2] subjects who watched videos of people speaking under stress experienced second-hand stress themselves! To be more specific, observers experienced differential changes in cardiac activity that were based on the speaker's stress level in the video being viewed.

The concept of a "stress contagion" even exists in the classroom. In a different study,[3] researchers found that stress

can be communicable: Higher levels of teacher burnout sig-
nificantly predicted students' increased stress levels, measured in terms of the students' cortisol levels. This just goes
to show that the occupational stress of our leaders can most
certainly "flow" to rest of us.

So, knowing there's a contagious aspect to stress, how
can you protect yourself? Here are three ways to shield
yourself from the negative.

1. **Check in on your safety.** The first thing I want you
   to do is to remind yourself of something foundational:
   You are safe and not in crisis. So go ahead and repeat
   that statement now: "I am safe." A work or relationship
   emergency might feel like a true crisis or life-threatening
   disaster, but plenty of the time, it is not! Remind yourself that you are physically okay and that this is not
   life or death.

2. **Create some distance from the stress source.** Let's say
   your coworker is a serious complainer. If you've set a
   limit and they absentmindedly forget it (or purposely
   ignore it), it's time to honor your own needs. You can
   create some distance by saying something like, "I'm
   doing my best to break up with complaining. Can we
   make a pact to not complain when we hang out? That
   would really help." This communicates your boundaries
   and sets the expectation that if complaining continues,
   you may distance yourself from the relationship. If it's
   not a coworker that's stressing you out, but a group
   dynamic, keep your interactions in those situations brief
   and be ready to make a quick exit so you're not stuck in
   a prolonged interaction.

3. **Formulate some physical feel-goods.** When you're
   in the thick of a stressful situation, it's reassuring to

anticipate a physical pleasure of some kind, even if it's small. So think about what little promise you can make to yourself, and follow through on, in a physical way. Is it a sanity-restoring bath, a guttural scream into your pillow, whacking the daylights out of a tennis ball, or a prolonged snuggle session with your pet? Make a date now to do that with yourself and then enjoy looking forward to it.

Just because stress can be passed on doesn't mean we need to turn in its direction or lean into it. Practice these strategies and before you know it, you'll have a toolbox of ways to unsubscribe from the stress of the noise around you. Insist on it!

 ## Sidestep Others' Negative Behavior

Hostility. Rudeness. Constant disrespect or criticism.

It's crucial to recognize—and then decline—other people's invitations to be negative. Now mind you, I'm not talking about occasional negativity like the very human need to vent once in a while. I'm talking about declining offers to engage in behavior that's constantly critical of people, predicts the worst, or for another reason, makes you deeply uncomfortable. So let's look at how to pass on negative behavior from downbeat colleagues, just like Andrea did with me.

First, choose whether or not you want to get drawn in. If you hear a colleague start on a negative rant, ask yourself if this conversation is worth engaging in. You only have so much energy to spend—and in some cases, it's not worth your effort to continue listening or get in a debate. Don't hesitate to remove yourself from the situation by getting up and attending to a different task or approaching someone whose company you do appreciate. You can also say, "I prefer to focus on the positives of XYZ" and excuse yourself.

Another approach is to challenge a colleague's negative view. When you do this, you're neutralizing the negative—and providing a more balanced perspective. If your colleague says, for example, "With the re-org happening, it's probably going to lead to layoffs for our division," you could say, "We don't know what's going to happen with the re-org. We've been kept in the loop so far—layoffs may happen, but they might not." Know that challenging your colleague's view doesn't necessarily convert them to your way of seeing things, but it may make them less likely to bring complaints to you in the future.

You can also bring the conversation back to what's in their control. When you refocus on what's doable—rather than what's negative and out of a person's hands—you remind people they can choose what they focus on. If, for example, your friend says, "We tried an initiative like this before, it will never work," you could remind them that they can play a role in making the initiative successful in the future. You might say, "What are your ideas for making it work?" or "How can your actions bring about success?"

Lastly, you can seek out more positive people. People often judge you based on the company you keep. So my question is, is your friend group reflective of the values that mean the most to you? If not, it's a great time to seek out more positive people, people who are encouraging and think in terms of possibilities. Doing that will empower you to spend your time with people who give and take positivity. And to choose more carefully who you allow in your inner circles.

Sometimes the most powerful move we can make in a negative situation is to stop subjecting ourselves to it—or to steer the conversation somewhere new. By using these tools, you can be thoughtful about how you handle negativity in your relationships. Because *you're in charge.* And you have so many better choices.

 ## The Problem with Energy-Matching

"Match that energy."

That's not only a popular saying on a t-shirt but a viral social media quote intended to remind people of a supposed power move they can make in their relationships. The idea is, when other people bring a salty, negative, or toxic mood—you mirror them, matching their same outward qualities. Some people view this as playing "offense," interpersonally, rather than defense.

I have an issue with that. In fact, more than one!

Look, when we're swimming the waters of a toxic workplace, it's understandable it can seem like a matter of daily survival to mimic the dynamics we see around us. If they're hypercompetitive, we better be too. If it's a high "blame" culture, we better be on a constant lookout for culprits. If it's a critical, harsh culture, we better add a thick layer of skin—and more of it. After all, we don't want to stand out as a poor culture fit or give people more reasons to pick on us! In situations like this, lots of people think, "I didn't invent the game, but I really need to figure out the rules and learn to play it."

Well, there are some very real dangers in mirroring *their* energy. Here are a few of them—so you can save yourself the stress and practice healthier ways of operating:

1. **It can feel really inauthentic.** Do you really want to look back one day and say, "I really excelled at being petty when that other person made cheap digs at me!"? Look, if you are fundamentally not a jerk, lowering yourself to the point of acting like one is not going to make you feel good or build your self-confidence. In fact, you'll have *more* toxic residue to scrub off yourself later if you match *their BS*. Instead, work harder to stay aligned to your top two or three values. Even if you feel like a misfit, you will have a healthy respect for yourself.

2. **Just because you acknowledge their way of being doesn't mean you need to accept it.** Let's say you work somewhere where yelling is the standard. When you take on those same noxious behaviors, you are co-signing those actions—endorsing them, even! Instead of copying what you see around you, acknowledge the truth of it mentally (and out loud if you have the where-withal). Realize that in this case, yelling back won't help anyone else or fix the underlying issue.

3. **Respond to their behavior by voting with your feet.** If you work in a place that is constantly trampling on your boundaries, values, or self-respect, I want to urge you to build a plan to leave. No one, and I repeat, *no one* is entitled to steal your dignity. Similarly, just because they grind and grind and grind doesn't mean you should *grind yourself* into dust. It's time to learn to love the sound of your feet walking away from garbage treatment.

When it comes to deeply toxic people and places, you do not need to act a part. If anything, you are deserving today—right now—to be spoken to and treated with respect. If there's anything that needs matching, remember, it should be what you give *and get* at work.

 ## Wipe Away What's Negative

I'm probably the last person you'd catch using a baseball analogy, but if the metaphor fits . . .

Not long ago my teenage nephew told me about a physical technique he learned that's helped his baseball game. I haven't been able to stop thinking about it or experimenting with it since. I think it can help you too.

The idea comes from H.A. Dorfman's *The Mental Game of Baseball*, a major premise of which is: if a player is stewing in negativity, they are toast. So, to help players vent their frustration (without getting stuck in it!), Dorfman recommends players do a physical gesture that allows them to feel and concentrate on their anger or upset, followed by a second gesture that allows them to let it go.

Wouldn't it be wonderful to have a tool like that at your disposal?

One of Dorfman's suggestions includes a player smoothing the dirt in the batter's box with their cleat, wiping away all negative thoughts or previous bad hits, and *then* stepping their foot in confidently before they bat. Another suggestion in a player's moment of anger is to pick up some grass, squeezing it and putting all your negative energy into it. After a beat, you throw the grass and your negative emotions out of the way.

What about you? The next time you're upset and want to regain your focus or composure, try these ideas—or better yet, tailor them and make them your own:

- **Pick up a touchstone:** Get yourself a handheld item that fits neatly in your palm—a smooth rock or stone, a tennis ball, or a small plastic bottle; think about keeping it in your desk drawer, bag, or home. Give yourself a few minutes as you transition out of one situation—and into another—to squeeze all your negative feelings into that object. As you squeeze, close your eyes for a moment to really lock in all that negativity into the object. Then totally relax your grip and put that object—and feeling—aside.

- **Massage your forearm:** If you're stewing on something upsetting, try massaging your forearm with moderate to vigorous pressure. Allow yourself to focus on your feelings of upset as you knead your muscle. Then as a second step, relax your arms on your arm rests, exhale loudly, and feel the release of negative emotion.

- **Tighten your muscles:** With progressive muscle relaxation, you slowly and systematically tense and tighten your muscles, followed by a rest. I like to do this by making my hands into tight-clenched fists, tightening my abs, followed by my thighs, calves, and toes. I then hold all those muscles clenched for about 10 seconds, feeling all my negative feelings, and then exhale and let go. This two-step process helps you release tension and feel a really clear contrast between stressed and non-stressed states.

- **Write in an unedited stream of consciousness:** Break open a notebook and go to town with your feelings. Remember, this isn't a third-grade history exam! You can write messy, in scrawl, in graffiti, and with colorful words (!). As you do, feel yourself imparting that negativity overload into your pen or pencil and then onto the page. When you're done, forcefully close the binder, notebook, or journal and breathe out deeply.

Honoring the feeling that *things suck right now* is an important way to honor yourself. And the really beautiful thing? You always have choices about how you react to the negative. If those feelings won't serve you right now—or you need to put them aside momentarily, give yourself permission to do exactly that. You have more control than you think!

Deflect Gossiping, Triangulating, and Complaining

If you've ever been stuck in the presence of a negative colleague, you know it can be tough, uncomfortable, and tiring. And, after hearing all of their gripes and disappointments, it probably makes you feel *more negative!* And that doesn't exactly help your confidence.

The truth is, there are ordinary, everyday behaviors that can be harmful to your relationships—and worse, your reputation. We're going to look at three specific kinds of risky behaviors. When you can recognize these negative behaviors for what they are—you can regulate your own actions better and avoid doing them. And you know what else? You can steer clear of negative people—this is important because negativity has been shown to lessen your intelligence—and memory,[4] even your immune system.[5] Remember, it's more than okay to be choosy about those close to you.

The first landmine to avoid is gossiping. Gossip is that casual chatter about other people that's usually speculative. And let's be real: it's often unflattering to the person being talked about. If you're gossiping—or you're befriending someone who's a known gossip—it's a quick way for you to lose credibility. People may assume you're unproductive—spending your time talking badly of others—and even worse, it can hurt people's trust in you. People may also think that if you gossip about others, you probably complain about them too.

Another risky behavior is triangulating. Triangulating is similar to venting—but the issue is, it's not done in the spirit of finding resolution. If we have a problem with a friend or colleague, everyone knows it's a good idea to address the issue directly with the person. But when we avoid doing that in favor of telling a third person about our problem, it becomes triangulating. Here, we're talking about someone else while avoiding them. The problem is that it can waste your time and allow the problem to keep festering. It can also diminish your integrity by getting back to the person you were talking about.

The last behavior we should address is complaining. When we regularly vocalize all the things that bother us, we can get a reputation as a complainer, a perception that tends to stick. The issue here is that people can start to think you don't take responsibility, chronically pinning the fault for things on others. Potential friends and acquaintances may also think you can't cope with change or that you're rigid or intolerant of ambiguity. Complaining almost always paints you in a negative light.

By knowing what behaviors can repel—rather than attract—friends, you can put the right foot forward instead. So think about what you convey to others—and the kind of people you surround yourself with. Commit to inspiring and lifting up others. Then, expect the same in return.

 ## Carve Out Time to Heal

"I just can't catch a break."

"I'm screwed."

"Bad bosses seem to crop up wherever I go."

A toxic job can create all kinds of distressing stories and headlines in our minds. In my own life, I've not only internalized negativity and carried it with me for a long time, a big part of me wondered if it was my own fault.

If you've just left a toxic job, particularly one that did a number on your self-esteem, here's my advice to help you move forward.

1. **Understand you need time to heal.** It may seem like your experience at one bad workplace will be fixed by moving on to a better one, but for so many of us, that's not enough! If you can, give yourself a pause, even a two-week buffer of time if you can, to recover between jobs. That can help you process what you went through and make a clear break with the pattern you were just in (people often describe this as survival mode, grinding away, or drudgery). No, your pain or suffering probably won't neatly fit into a schedule and then be done, but even acknowledging that you need some healing time will buy you some extra patience and self-compassion.

2. **Validate your worth.** Using your time off (even if you can only manage a long weekend!), it's time to start building your self-esteem back up. You probably

took some mental and emotional blows in your job, so this is a time to *do the opposite*. You can start by making a "Reasons I'm awesome" list where you make a top 10 list of things you like about yourself. Or you can storyboard some of your biggest strengths and accomplishments over the last 10 years, so you can start to feel good again. You can build on this by taking some self-assessments focused on identifying your strengths that highlight your unique gifts.

3. **Make a plan for how a different job or career could better line up with your values and boundaries.** You most certainly deserve good treatment. Now, how do you plan to go about getting it? Maybe for one person, that means actively looking for a job with reasonable hours or remote options. For someone else, it might mean making a point to find a friendly culture where people are supportive, complementary, or helpful to each other. Just like with buying a house, we all have our nice-to-have list and our nonnegotiable list. It's the same with your next career step. Take some time now to list out three to five features that are a must for you in a next role, and separate them from a second column you make about what's nice to have. Examples for either list could include: excellent pay, the chance to further your education, a track record of efforts around inclusion, room to grow, a collaborative culture, healthy hours, a doable (or nonexistent) commute, strong benefits, or a meaningful mission.

Now that you know how to make a comeback, with plenty of (self) support, guess what? You can help someone else going through the same thing! Seriously though, if you're anything like me, talking openly about toxic experiences has helped me heal in ways I never imagined. I like to think it can help someone else who is feeling stuck, alone, and desperate. As you hear others share their experiences of toxicity, believe them, validate them, and support and encourage them.

You are so much more than your toxic experience, don't forget it!

Address a Work Friend's Negative Behavior

Have you ever been in a work situation where a colleague said something in poor taste—or something that was outright wrong? Did it make you cringe? Just about all of us have been there. It can take courage to address a coworker's negative behavior and a swiftness to address it there in the moment.

But when people fail to address negative behavior, they sidestep addressing their own feelings. They also miss out on deepening the honesty and respect of a healthy relationship. **So, let's look at four techniques for confronting unseemly behavior in a colleague.**

First, ask them to explain their comment. If a friend makes a joke, for example, that's offensive to a particular group, you can speak up and ask them to clarify what they mean. You can say "Why'd you say that?" or "I'm not seeing the humor here. What do you mean?" When you do this, you're prompting them to clarify their remark, which is important in case their comment simply came out wrong.

The second technique you can use is to *be a mirror*. To do this, paraphrase the gist of what you just heard. You might say, "Jennifer, I hear you painting an entire group in

a derogatory way. Is that what you mean to say?" Playing it
back this way—as you're hearing it—gives the other person
one more chance to clear up their stance.

**You could also explain how this behavior is out of
sync with their decent, respectable side.** If this person is
your friend, then they most likely have some virtues you
respect. By calling out some of those virtues, you can appeal
to their positive nature, showing how this comment is jar-
ring or out of character. You might say, "Raj, I've always
seen you as open-minded and fair, so I'm upset to hear you
speak this way."

**And finally, ask them to stop doing it in front of
you.** Whether or not your friend sees things as you do in
the end, it's important for you to take a stand. So don't be
afraid to assertively state your need. You might say, "John,
please don't make remarks like this in my presence" or
"I'm asking you to stop making negative comments about
X in front of me." As awkward as this might feel, you're
letting your friend know where an important line is for
you—so they can change their behavior and start to respect
your limits.

Our actions in everyday moments define what we stand
for. And we teach others about ourselves by what we accept,
reject, and reinforce. So be the one to challenge unseemly
behavior. If not you, then who?

 ## Use Your Container

When you're right in the throes of navigating a toxic situation or dynamic, wouldn't it be wonderful to know that you

could hold space for that experience—*without* it taking over your life? (Unlike the awful situation I described earlier in my own career, where my work experience bled into every other facet of my life!)

If you're having a hard time handling your distress, I can't urge you enough to go to therapy. That can be transformative for learning to cope, manage, and heal through hard experiences. Not to mention, it can help you thoughtfully choose something different.

In addition to taking mental health action on your own behalf, I want to introduce you to the container exercise. What's really cool about the container exercise is that allows you to take what's upsetting you and keep it safe, without living those feelings every moment.

So imagine this scenario: you are struggling in a job you hate, in a work culture you hate even more—one that's full of backstabbing, egos, and favoritism. Just this morning, someone undermined you, cutting you out of important conversations and you. Feel. Heated! Not only is there a churning sensation inside you, you *also* want to punch something in the outside world. (Maybe even the offender's face. You can be honest!)

Knowing you were planning to take your upcoming lunch break outside, in a beautiful park, you decide you would like to table these angry feelings for a time and enjoy your lunch and mental break from work. This is a perfect moment for the container exercise! To do this, follow these steps:

1. **Imagine a secure container in your mind's eye.** As you conjure up an image that works for you, I want you to focus on this container being strong enough to hold big,

sometimes wild feelings. What could properly hold that? A wooden crate? A shipping container? A beautiful, ornate metal box? You decide. My container looks like a carved wood, teak box from India.

2. **Now imagine taking some upsetting images or "movies" from your life and putting them in the container.** Is there any else you're missing that you want to add? Some things that have been weighing on you or eating at you? Go ahead and add those too. I like to picture these going in as printed photographs of upsetting things or little old-fashioned movie reels.

3. **The next step is to close it.** Knowing your container will safely hold some of your most burdensome, messy, difficult feelings, it's time to put a lid on it. As you shut the door securely, think about if you want to add anything else to make your container that much more secure—maybe it's the placement of it, a lock put on it, or something else. All right, go ahead and do that now.

As you focus on this container keeping your feelings safe and sound, know you can revisit it or open it at any time. You can practice over time, opening your box, sorting through its contents, and processing it so you can move on. You can also practice filling your container and storing it away so you can fully show up for the moments that matter to you (maybe saving it for your next therapy session!). With every new tool you learn, you're that much closer to having a "Swiss army knife" of techniques for managing even the hardest people and environments. Here's to skilling up!

Decide You'll Be a Light

Can you picture a sweet little second grader sitting in the cafeteria—eyes roaming around the room for a buddy—while they eat lunch all alone? If you can relate at all to this experience, it probably felt lousy, didn't it? The thing about that kid is, it doesn't take a village to change his experience, or even a group—it only takes one person to say, "Hey, can I join you?" or "Want to come sit with me?"

How simple, yet heroic, an action!

Well, you can be that heroic person too. That light when everything else is *ghastly dark*.

On a basic level, we human beings want to feel like we're part of a collective. We're practically wired neuro-scientifically to be members of a "tribe." Some scientists even liken our need to connect socially with our need for food and water![6]

That's why, as part of your own mission to be a light for others, it's so important to establish teams and friend groups who are welcoming, accessible, and open. How can you do this?

First, be an ally to a newcomer. Being the new person or outsider, as we've established, can be scary. So *be quick* to lend your support to a newcomer who does join your group or company. You can tell them you're really glad they came, you can validate the idea they put forward, or you could speak well of them to others. By showing up for them in this way, you can boost their positive interaction and ensure they'll want to come back!

Now, decide you'll include others in decisions that affect them. Nobody likes a dictator or someone who belittles their experience and skills. So make a promise to yourself that you'll involve people—survey them, talk to them, ask for their best ideas—when it comes to implementing a change that will touch them or their work. This gives a sense of group membership to everyone—and *invites them in*. As you go, encourage fresh views and involvement, even if it differs from the way things have always been done.

Next, give people permission to be human. If you don't manage people today, you probably will at some point in the future. Here's a tip: they will have vulnerable, messy, deeply uncomfortable moments in their lives. Whether they catch an illness and can't easily get back on their feet, or have a special needs child, or a depressive episode—or something else—*meet them where they are*. Send the message that *that's okay*! Be accepting of the fact that people don't produce robotic output and show people compassion when they are caught off guard or struggling.

Hey, we've all been the quiet voice or new person—or the one who wanted to belong—at some point. When you bring compassion and light to the experience of your teammates, *they will never forget it*. Open up your teams and friend groups to others, and you open up the door to a world of possibilities.

8 Rise above Fails and Setbacks

Sometimes I think it's a miracle I got an MBA.

Just one week after I started my program, I had written out my "I quit" email to the business school director. I told a classmate and friend I was quitting too. My justification? "I'm just not a great fit here."

By "here" I meant surrounded by very smart, self-assured businesspeople from all different industries. I was certain they read corporate financial statements and *The Wall Street Journal—for fun*. Me, on the other hand? I practically had an allergy to math and extremely limited financial experience.

I was also the only person in the program coming from a social work background. That gave me a sense that not only was I out of my depth, but I might not be taken seriously either.

"Cut your losses," I told myself. "You don't really fit. Just quit and be done with it."

Well, what I can see clearly now is that "fit" was not the problem.

Intimidation was.

In that moment, my fear of embarrassment and failure was massive, so much so that it eclipsed my dream of getting my degree. I felt straight up insecure! On a loop, I kept thinking, "You can't do this. You're going to struggle and humiliate yourself for two years."

As I look back now, I can see I was harping on everyone else's potential—and completely underestimating my own.

At the end of that first week, weary from anxiety, I said to myself, "Selena, just give it one more week." After all, I had dreamed of going to business school for ages. Being at Johns Hopkins University was a big deal to me. And I had put time, effort, and energy into applying—not to mention the other people who had vouched for me via recommendations and the school leaders who had seen promise in me and gave me a spot.

And so I did—I gave it one more week. And then another. I started chipping away at the everyday projects and challenges I was given, and somehow *the weeks I survived* started to rack up. Ultimately, I kept giving it *one more week* until two years later . . . I made it.

There I stood, leading the commencement procession of dozens of other students—all 5 foot 2 inches of me— carrying this historic school's gigantic, heavyweight flagpole, on the stage of a beautiful auditorium in downtown Baltimore. I was appointed that year's Student Marshall, a role given to one student by faculty to represent the student class in this exciting new milestone.

No one was more shocked than me, particularly because I finished with a 4.0 GPA and a second-year scholarship award for my academic performance. *Me*, who had panicked during the math part of the SAT and started randomly filling in bubbles! Even better than any school honor was that I ended up making lifelong, cherished friends. When I try to picture my life without those relationships, without everything I learned in those two years—well, I'm *very grateful* I didn't send that "I quit" email.

What no one could have prepared me for was this lesson: pushing through fear is *how* you gain confidence. You don't wait 'til there's no trepidation to act! Maybe the biggest surprise is that today, having that MBA—even if it's completely meaningless to someone else or just a piece of paper—I feel what I'd describe as *earned confidence*! I fought for my ability to size up a company's operating model and to properly read a financial statement. I had to summon every ounce of courage to give presentation after presentation on video. I had to stand on the edge of my comfort zone *and trust myself*. And you know what? My body and mind won't soon forget that.

Years later, when a journalist asked me what advice I had for my younger self, it was an easy answer: "Make more faceplants, screwups, and mistakes. Stop being so scared to fail. Start taking risks knowing you might make a mess!" Today, I am far from a Jedi master at this. But I keep requiring myself to look for the spark of my best ideas (and if I hadn't, this book wouldn't even exist!), and then to act on them, even with the uncertainty and pain of knowing they might go sideways.

Whether your biggest challenge with failure is anticipating it, avoiding it, or recovering from it—this chapter is all about helping you through. You'll learn mind, body, and interpersonal techniques that prompt you to think twice when you're tempted to pull the plug on something out of intimidation. After all, what would it mean to give it one more day, one week, or one month while *you* suspend judgment?

You'll also learn how to handle one of the more painful kinds of fails—rejection. Because even in the moments we feel most powerless, we really do have the chance to frame—and reframe—the situation.

We'll also look together at that prickly, sour experience called jealousy. Comparing ourselves to others (especially in the social media age) and coming up short is *very* common and can feel like a very real setback. And we'll address regrets, since we all have a few. How do you manage those—and going a step further—forgive yourself for them?

And my favorite of all, we'll explore how to launch a comeback in the face of a setback or fail. Sometimes even the most final of verdicts can be rewritten or reimagined. You'll learn to bring some healthy skepticism to the "final word" and to invent new potential endings.

Remember, mess-ups, pain, and remorse are not bad things. The point of a well-lived life isn't to sidestep these experiences, it's to learn and graduate from them, amassing confidence and self-assurance as you do. Here's to making some beautiful messes!

 ## Color-Code Your Approach

"How did your interview go?"

"It was kind of a fail. . . . I mean, it started out well, but then things went sideways when they started to ask me questions about things I don't know."

I have heard so many variations of this phrase from people who went on a job interview (which is just one example of a high-stakes situation)—more variations than Lady Gaga has wigs!

Look, we all have those moments when we go from being *in the flow*—demonstrating really strong performance—to those moments where we're in a shaky, unsteady zone. Where it feels like we could straight up fail.

Here's something I wish I'd known sooner: we are *not stuck* in these shaky states!

The key—and I'm talking about a big, antique, supersecret skeleton key that unlocks a holy grail—is learning to notice what zone you're in *right now*. Then, you can apply a few tips to steer yourself to a better place. By color-coding your performance in an important situation, you can keep yourself performing optimally and feed your self-confidence! For the sake of making this process clear, I'm going to use a job interview as our example. Here's what I mean:

- **When you're in the green zone, you're open and receptive to new ideas, connected to the people around you, and in the flow.** In a job interview specifically, this might feel like relying comfortably on the talking points you've prepared in advance, making strong, engaging eye contact with your interview panel, and smiling naturally throughout the conversation. It feels great to be in the green zone, and this is a place you want to reliably steer the conversation!

- **In the yellow zone, just like at a yellow traffic light, you might experience hesitation and move with caution.** You may even feel some discomfort. In a job interview, this might happen after starting out in the green zone, but then you get asked a question you don't feel prepared for. That curveball question can easily lead you to self-doubt. Outwardly, the yellow zone in this scenario might sound like "Uh . . . ummm . . . well see . . . uh. . . . <*Gulp*>." Inwardly, your thought process might sound something like a panicked, "Why on earth can't I think of something to say?! For the love of all that's good and merciful, why can't my mind think of an answerrrrr?!" But let me assure you, this is not doomsday! Noticing you're in the yellow zone is the first step to guiding yourself back to green. As you most likely notice your heart rate quicken, palms itch, or armpits sweat, you might ask the other party to restate or reexplain their question. Or you could lead with *what you do know*. If you're asked something very tricky or complex you could start by saying, "Here's what I can tell you about X" and simply start there. If you don't take an active hand in noticing you're in the yellow zone, it can escalate into a red zone!

- **In a red zone, we often stop the flow of the conversation or connection either because the conversation becomes stunted or because we have shut down or retreated.** Outwardly, this might look like a long gap in silence, panicked eye contact, and everyone's favorite, uncontrollable sweating. Inwardly, this might feel like we're fixated on how wrong it's going, *we believe our self-doubts* and maybe even start to self-attack. The inside voice might be saying, "Why did I ever think I could get a job doing X?! This is a disaster." *Yeesh*. But even in the red zone, you are not stuck. This is a great time to notice you feel "off" but to give no more attention than that to your negative thoughts. Then, take a deep, reassuring breath, and plant your feet down firmly on the floor to ground yourself and spread out your toes. You can say to yourself, "I'm safe, I'm supported, I'm breathing, and I can move myself back to green." Then, start with one firm action. So if they say, "Tell me about your style as a supervisor," and you weren't expecting that—you could start with the area you're most versed in, by saying for example, "Ahh yes—one of the things about supervising I most enjoy is [X aspect], which I approach with [Y method] . . ." Answering the easiest part of the question or the one you're most experienced or comfortable with gives you the momentum to steer you back to green!

	Green zone	Yellow zone	Red zone
Looks like	• Being open, flexible, relaxed, "in the flow," and connected to your audience	• Cautious, hesitant, unsure, caught off guard	• Stopped, stunted, stuck
What to do when you're in it	• Notice you're in the green and feel good about it (or notice a specific positive move you made and feel good about it)	• Ask for clarification or for them to restate the question • Lead with what you *do know*	• Plant your feet firmly on the floor, spread out your toes, and feel the support and ground beneath you

(continued)

(*Continued*)

Green zone	Yellow zone	Red zone
• Keep tuning into your audience to read their shifting interest, discomfort, curiosity, etc.	• Take a deep breath in and picture inhaling clarity and comfort • Take a drink to buy a moment or pause • Make a body shift in your chair to mark a physical and mental reset; a purposeful move back to the green zone	• Put your shoulders back and inhale slowly to reassure your body you're okay • Crowd out/ refuse to give negative thoughts focus or attention • Restate the question in your own words and then answer *your* question • Break a question or problem into parts and address one part at a time • Start answering the easiest part of the question

Do you see how you could apply this cool system to other situations such as giving a presentation, pitching your business, or facilitating an important meeting—so you can avoid failure in the first place? You can even give yourself a visual reminder by bringing a green pen, having red, yellow, and green Post-its in your bag, or by bringing along a green folder.

When you're tuned into yourself, you can tap into your best focus. You're at the wheel of driving the conversation forward with the ability to shift up or down, or side to side, as needed. Go forward and triumph!

Have a Short Memory

One of the lessons that's most helped me to stay married is this: have a short memory for the little stuff.

And you know what? It also applies to life's little fails and disappointments!

I'm not talking about overlooking massive rifts, flaws, or dysfunctions, mind you. What I mean is that when there's silly, small-scale stuff you *could* get worked up about, crumbs on the kitchen counter or someone putting your keys where they're hard to find, decide purposely that you're going to drop it and move on. That means out of care and concern about your relationship, as well as for your own energy and sanity: You. Let. It. Go.

Coping with your own little flaws and botched moments in life is no different. You could hold on to every awkward encounter you've had or smolder over that time you worded something oddly or ineloquently when speaking up in a meeting, but it won't serve you! When it comes to our littler fails, it's a great habit to learn to brush it off.

Three of my favorite ways to let things go include doing these physical actions:

- **Shrug your shoulders, smile, and simultaneously say, "So sue me!" "So what?!" or "Big freaking deal!"** The idea here is, rather than exaggerate "your crime" by prosecuting it to the fullest extent of the law, you minimize it. Phrases such as "So what?" are a quick reminder to your body and mind that this is not front-page news. That helps you avoid overfocusing on your faux pas or putting yourself on trial.

- **Write down your mess-up in disappearing ink.** Rather than making a mental tattoo of whatever you did wrong (or creating a mental screening room that replays your mess-up over and over!), try this (you might just feel like a student at Hogwarts!). Close your eyes and picture writing down your mistake in blue ink, in no more than one sentence. After writing it, look at it, and watch it fade away into invisibility, never to be seen again.

- **Find the funny.** I know the last thing you might want to do after making a mistake is laugh. But here's my challenge to you: Is there something even a little absurd that you could make light of regarding your mistake? Is the typo you made in that email actually a silly sounding word? (I once wrote "Dead Michael" instead of "Dear Michael" to a prospect! Oof!) When you reached out to give someone a hug and they hesitated and shook your hand back, was that like a funny master-class on how to give an awkward greeting? When you can find the silliness and humor in your error, you can much more quickly own it and move on.

Even the most famous fails—experienced by people who failed before they succeeded—among the likes of Thomas Edison, Arianna Huffington, Vera Wang, and Stephen King—yielded more positives than negatives, thanks to their screwups or setbacks.

Every time you make a little screwup, it's proof that you're human—just like everyone else. *You* decide what place it occupies in your life. Remember, it takes a powerful person to take themselves lightly!

 ## How to Deal with Being Intimidated

What was the *most memorable thing* about interviewing 50+ C-level women leaders over the years for my books? In first place were the raw, eye-opening leadership gems and insights these leaders shared with me. But a close second place—something I can remember viscerally—was the intimidation factor of sitting down with these heavyweights! Even though I had reached out to these leaders and they said yes to interviews, I felt acutely aware of how much more they were. But I knew if I got too fixated on their status, I could've failed in those interviews to ask the good questions or make real connections.

Do you ever find yourself intimidated by certain people? It might be a super self-confident person you kind of admire. Or maybe it's a bit of a scary figure who makes you feel unsettled. Maybe it's a powerful authority whose rank has you feeling lots of pressure.

Well, rather than let that feeling take you down, make you feel less than, or fail, there's a way you can reframe that

intimidation to take the edge off. Here are some quick confidence tips to "un-intimidate" yourself:

- **See them doing the ordinary.** One of the most
  grounding reminders when you're dealing with someone who intimidates you is this. Remember, they are
  human. Like you, they do ordinary, everyday things.
  So if you were getting ready to interview Oprah (how's
  that for a high-stakes moment!), you could remind
  yourself of five to seven things Oprah had to do today
  that you did, too. Some simple examples might include
  overcoming inertia to get out of bed, deciding what to
  wear, and eating something for breakfast. Try to have
  a little fun with this! Maybe while you picture them
  selecting their breakfast, you imagine they really want
  something yummy and decadent like chocolate chip
  pancakes but like you, they settle on something a little more sensible and wholesome. See how this brings
  them back down to earth a bit? Now try making a list
  like this about someone who intimidates you.

- **Tell yourself they're different, not intimidating.** If
  someone intimidates you, try making this mental shift.
  Instead of chalking it up to the fact that they might
  have more status, attribute it to difference—you are
  simply *different* from the other person. That doesn't
  make them better than you. Maybe they walk into
  a room and say their name at a volume of eight and
  you're still working on getting up to a volume of five.
  Rather than attribute bad or good to each person's style,
  simply remark how they're *different*.

- **Do the "Just like me" exercise.** Next time someone
  intimidates you, think about some of the same difficult or vulnerable emotions they feel, *just like you*. For

example, you could say, "This person has felt hopeful/ useless/lonely/scared . . . just like me" or "This person has woken up on the wrong side of the bed . . . just like me" or "This person has needed to summon courage to take action . . . just like me." Notice how this recalibrates your intimidation and makes them a regular person again?

What I've noticed is that intimidating types don't tend to lead with their flaws. That doesn't mean they don't have them. They definitely do! But they don't tend to be terribly self-deprecating or give people lots of fodder for criticizing them (they've usually mastered the last tip and easily let go of their own small fails!). They're often better at accentuating what *they do know*, what is working, and their strengths. So even if their faults aren't on full display, trust that they're there. None of us are infallible—even that person who makes your knees shake.

Intimidation is a natural experience we all face from time to time. As you deal with it, make sure you don't ignore your own accomplishments and positives in favor of *theirs*. Stand tall in your power, and remember they have the human capacity, just like you, to be vulnerable, to learn and evolve, to fail and shine.

Tangibly Release the Failure

If you've felt the hurt of a "No" (is there a rare unicorn among us who hasn't?!), you can probably relate to how easy it is to wallow in that rejection. Even if someone rejects you in the gentlest possible way, it can feel as if you're 20 feet

deep in a dark well of despair. Alone. Feeling like you were
Dismissed with a big capital "D."

Dwelling on your failure certainly feels bad. But here's
something you might not know: internalizing your failures actually reinforces neural pathways in your brain[1] that
expect more failure! Through what's called "the neuroplas-
tic response," the brain strengthens the circuits used most
frequently, which actually enhances their speed.

Whoa, right? I'm going to take a gamble and bet that
you don't want to strengthen your brain's wallowing muscles. Well, here's the best part of this research: it works both
ways! What we habitually practice creates efficiency in our
brains, allowing them to modify connections or rewire
itself. Knowing this, let's look at some physical ways to let
go of a failure, so you can make room for new, positive
pathways in your life.

Start here:

- **Expel it:** Close your eyes and picture exhaling your
  rejection or failure. As you take five deep breaths, really
  imagine your mistake totally leaving your system. For
  me, I tend to feel my failure as heaviness, and I like
  to watch as my breaths and body become lighter with
  exhalations. Start to picture your setback fully exiting
  your system, and watch it go away without resistance.

- **Do something well:** After exhaling your disappointment, it's a great time to set your brain up for the
  positive. So here's what I want you to do: purposefully
  tackle a small, achievable task you know you can do
  well. That is a crucial step to regaining confidence.
  Maybe it's cleaning your room with gusto—or exercis-
  ing hard—or pulling the daylights out of the weeds
  in your garden. That positive experience and sense of

knowing accomplishment will help you start to expect more positive things.

- **Cast it away:** I recommend you find a physical release to symbolize letting go of your botched fill-in-the-blank. Maybe it's burning a rejection letter in your BBQ (!), or throwing a stone in a creek to consciously let yourself feel a release. It could even mean taking a seed and planting it to represent a new kind of growth. It's powerful to our minds to act out the sensations of letting go—but how you do this can be totally individual. You get to decide what feels like healthy growth to you.

- **Create a smile file:** One of my favorite self-care hacks of all time, a smile file can truly take your worst day or mood and make it better. A smile file is a little personal collection of things that makes you feel great. It could include accolades, photos, letters, or notes, an award, a funny meme—you get the picture. You could make an email or digital version, but I personally like touching and sorting through each item. I have a simple manila folder that includes a picture of my best girlfriends and me in rainbow-colored wigs, a sonogram of my twins, a little love letter my husband wrote me, a letter from my publisher congratulating me on my first book—you get the idea. Look, we all need a little pick-me-up sometimes. Start your smile file, and remind yourself of all the tremendous good in your life.

When we learn to let go of those aching disappointments, we clean up our minds and hearts—and make space for new and better things. Just because the past didn't go according to plan doesn't mean the future can't be better than you ever imagined.

Manage the Jealousy Monster

Sigh. Ever felt a pang of jealousy when a work peer performed better than you?

I know, I know—we're supposed to celebrate each other's accomplishments. But sometimes you just can't help feeling that you wish it was *you* getting the "congratulations!"

I'm not proud of it, but I've certainly felt jealous of a colleague:

Years ago, I had a straightforward, professional presentation I was getting ready to give at a huge conference. I arrived an hour early and happened to catch the speaker before me.

My jaw almost hit the floor—she was amazing. Her story was compelling, she integrated upbeat music, she even ran around, weaving through the audience! She was a 12 out of 10 in her energy level and delivery.

I realized right away my academic presentation was going to be *very different* from hers. Like dry crackers after having ceviche—*bleh*. While I've since grown through this experience, on that day it stung to think about how we stacked up to each other.

If you have moments like this again and again, your confidence can take a hit—along with your morale, motivation, and job satisfaction. So what can you do?

The best way to pull yourself up is to put your envy in perspective.

That means looking at what you *can* control—things such as sharpening your skills, working hard with what you do have, and showing up to work every day a little bit better than you were yesterday. After all, you're in this position today because others recognize *your* value.

So even if people around you shine particularly brightly—or the environment you're in doesn't give you the validation you hope for—it's still important to confidently reaffirm your value for *yourself.*

These tips are for anyone who feels outshined by the people around them!

- **Seek a mentor in someone who's winning.** If someone is where you want to be, a productive (but sometimes counterintuitive) approach is to reach out and learn from them. What could you do to applaud their success and at the same time engage them to learn about their process? Ask them to grab lunch or coffee with you, or for a virtual conversation to understand their path to getting really good at "X." I like to be really transparent in these meeting requests so there's no mystery around "what the meeting's about." Then, you can ask how they got to where they are today and how you can follow in their footsteps.

- **Pick up some new skills.** Is your peer being celebrated for something outside of your skill set? If so, don't stew in jealousy. Instead, get smarter! Think about how you could invest in and expand your own domain knowledge. You don't necessarily have to mimic learning what your peer knows, but stop and reflect on what training or experience could enrich the value you already bring today. Similarly, you could focus on a cutting-edge part of your field that you would like to learn more about and become associated with. Pour your energy there!

- **Repeat "They have their Story, I have mine . . ."**
  Blogger Justin Zoradi offers up this brilliant advice, and
  I've used it many times. Our lives don't progress like
  swim lanes at the Olympics, where we're competing
  on a clock and only one winner can emerge. Our lives
  bob, weave, and zigzag at different rates. When you
  realize this, envying others can start to look (a) illogi-
  cal, and (b) ridiculous! So remind yourself, "There is no
  comparison" and "I'm working on becoming the best
  version of me." Lastly, when you're feeling envious and
  wishing you had someone else's success, you can ask
  yourself, "Would I really want to trade places with that
  person if I had to take all their baggage, too?"

Taking ownership and action on what you can directly
influence is one of the best ways to feel more confident.
And the same is true for learning new things and expand-
ing your skillset. With all of these new things you're going
to learn, you'll be more valuable to your company, more
impressive to your peers, and position yourself for new
opportunities and visibility.

 ## Finding Motivation in the Face of Ruts

How many times have we all thought to ourselves, "I'll start
that new habit on Monday"? Whether it's eating healthier
or moving our bodies more, we tend to overemphasize what
we can do in the future, glossing past what we can do *right
now*. Of course, that hurts our motivation because delaying
our own efforts assigns them to an unknown time in the
future. It also clears us of any accountability to act today.
Uh—not good.

Through coaching and training professional after professional, I've found there are three Ps, or pitfalls—based on our mindset: when we *procrastinate*, *protect*, or try to *perfect* something. These are common forms of delaying tasks that derail your progress—and undermine your goals. But by learning about these pitfalls, you can recognize when each one is happening. Then you can change course and try a better way forward. Let's take a look.

1. **The first P is when we procrastinate.** The procrastination I'm talking about isn't rare or exceptional—it's the chronic avoidance of an important task. And it's one of the biggest drains on our self-motivation. When we put things off, we feel badly about not starting, triggering a cycle of stress, which may de-motivate us even more from jumping in and getting started. A better way is to ask yourself these simple questions about your task:

   - What's one thing I can get started on right now?

   - What's the consequence if I don't do this now?

2. **The second P is when we attempt to protect ourselves by delaying an action.** Protecting comes from wanting to avoid potential pain, embarrassment, or the discomfort of taking a risk. But if you delay work in the name of protecting yourself, it's actually a form of self-sabotage. By hedging, you give yourself less time to complete your work, creating a shorter, more high-stakes, pressurized timeline. You'll get better results by asking yourself these questions:

   - What would make me feel more safeguarded in doing this task?

   - What is the absolute worst that can happen if I do it and jump in?

3. **The third P is when we try to perfect.** By trying to get a project just perfect, or feeling pressure to do it without a flaw, we can feel paralyzed to take action. Believe me, as a recovering perfectionist, I am an *expert* at this. But having such a high bar hurts our motivation. It can make us feel we're living up to an impossible standard. So we delay taking action so as not to disappoint anyone—including ourselves. But this approach sucks away all our creative license to do great work. Instead, a better way forward is to ask yourself these simple questions:

- What's required for me to do high-quality, rather than perfect, work on this?
- What can I do to feel a sense of pride in delivering on this work?

Motivation pitfalls that cause you to put off starting work are a lot like safety blankets. You may think they're providing comfort—or shielding you from outside embarrassment or failure. But they're actually pretty flimsy defense mechanisms. And the thing is, you're a lot stronger than you realize. Now that you know the common pitfalls of motivation, you can recognize them for what they are when they happen. Bring that new perspective with you. Then learn, and pivot toward your goals.

 ## Decide You'll "Fail Forward"

Ever made a disaster of a mistake? Like one where you didn't want to show up at work the next day?

I once wrote an important email to an executive I wanted to impress. Right after I hit "Send," I realized

I'd written the entire email in the subject line. I felt *scorched* with mortification! But while mistakes can certainly bruise our confidence, we're never alone when we make them. In fact, research finds that the average American worker makes 118 mistakes per year—about one every three days![2]

How can you stop skewering yourself after you've made a mistake? What I've learned from coaching thousands of emerging leaders is that they *negotiate a new direction for their failures.* They fail *forward.*

When people fail and then make another attempt—a do-over with more experience about what to avoid—they can write a new ending to their *mistake story.* This motivates us to act boldly in the future.

Frankly, failure is inevitable. So *prepare* to fail sometimes. What matters more than your mistakes is how you turn them into stepping stones for future success.

Use these tips to fail forward:

1. **Decide that the failure itself isn't the final word.**
   When I delivered leadership training for a consulting firm, one woman stood up and shared how she had failed miserably at a quantitative stretch assignment. But instead of cowering or hiding afterward, she asked leaders if she could take another stab at it. With more experience on what to avoid, she delivered the assignment capably and was told she "knocked it out of the park." If you're dealing with a fixable failure (which I'd argue most are)—be dogged that you'll write a new ending to the story. Raise your hand and ask for a do-over. It'll fuel your motivation to do well.

2. **Seek someone out to normalize the experience.** When I delivered a negotiation workshop at a large company,

I asked a group how they coped with rejection. One woman, Rachel, explained that when she negotiated a raise, she was really disappointed to get a "no." She went directly to her car, cried, and proceeded to mentally steep in her failure for the next two or three weeks. She told *no one*. Then another woman, Swati, shared the aftermath of her own failed negotiation. When she got a "no" answer, she immediately approached a mentor at her company. Swati's mentor said the "no" was normal and not personal to her. Rachel was sidelined for weeks by the failed negotiation. Swati bounced back right away. The lesson? Consult someone more seasoned or tenured than you, and let them give you their read of your "failure." You'll be inspired to go back and ask again.

3. **Share it as learning for the greater good.** When you experience a setback and then incorporate it into your own toolbox of leadership, it's really hard for other people to use it against you. Why not share a story with your team about a misstep or mistake you made so that others can learn from it and do better? Not only will it prompt other people to feel safe sharing about their mistakes, it gives you a chance to show people your path to learning *a better way*. When you share your own mess-ups with others, you show that you can survive those bumps and even better, use them to your advantage to grow stronger.

Even your most mortifying work mistake is "get-over-able." The more you see it as part of the fabric of the human experience, the quicker you'll find yourself on the other side of it.

Forgive Yourself and Let Go of the Past

A missed job opportunity. A botched business partnership. A decision not to pursue your education further. A chance to build your brand that you didn't take.

Any one of these events can cause us to ruminate on what we *should* have done.

To an extent, that's good! Reflecting on past actions to determine where improvement can be made, and then letting go, is a healthy part of self-development.

It's when we dwell on things that can't be changed and perpetually beat ourselves up for past missteps that our confidence and potential for success will suffer a major blow. As the saying goes, (and just like the title of Dr. Chris Thurman's book) "Stop should-ing all over yourself!"

Whether or not it's convenient, forgiving yourself for your past is essential to moving forward in life.

Why?

Well, for a start, constantly ruminating on our past leaves us *stuck* there.

The guilt we feel often prevents us from seeing the truth: that we are worthy people deserving of forgiveness, peace, and happiness.

How about you?

Have you ever noticed you're quick to encourage other people to forgive themselves? Do you constantly reassure people that it's "totally okay" and then forget their slip even happened?

Why don't we extend this same forgiveness and compassion toward ourselves? Why do we beat ourselves up for days, weeks, months, even years for our past mistakes?

It's time we start learning how to forgive ourselves as quickly as we would forgive anyone else. Try these tips to do just that.

Tips for moving on from your past:

1. **Take responsibility and find the lesson.** Forgiving yourself is about more than just moving on. It's about acknowledging your past behaviors and accepting what happened. Taking responsibility for what you've done can bring an incredible sense of relief and help you release guilt and shame. But here's what really takes it to the next learning level: I want you to identify the *one big lesson* from your regret that you want to impress in your mind for the future. Some example lessons might include: don't be so quick to underestimate what you can do in a challenging new situation, or don't instinctively place others' input above your own instinct or judgment.

2. **See forgiveness as a vitamin.** There's a reason we want to avoid feeling shameful or angry: it literally hurts! Karen Swartz, MD, director of the Mood Disorders Adult Consultation Clinic at Johns Hopkins Hospital, says chronic anger puts you into a fight-or-flight mode, which results in changes in heart rate, blood pressure, and immune response. Those changes then increase the risk of depression, heart disease, and diabetes among other conditions. Dr. Swartz says forgiveness, on the other hand, calms stress levels, leading to improved health.[3] Instead of seeing forgiveness as an indulgence, see it as a fortifier and vitamin for your health.

3. **Repair damage and rebuild trust.** Apologizing for your mistake is the first step to repairing damage and rebuilding trust. You might need to apologize to yourself in

some cases. This is an important step because it shows you want to remedy the issue and you want to do better. Making an effort to repair things fuels a sense of positivity and rebuilding; it turns a page from where things were to a new page. You'll see it becomes a whole lot easier to forgive yourself when you feel like you've done everything you can do to make things right, or at least better.

Remember, the human emotion of remorse is not a bad thing. While it's not a fun feeling, it indicates you are a good person who doesn't want to hurt people, do bad things, or play small in your own life.

Squeeze the juice out of that regret and decide you'll use it to make more positive choices in the future.

Have the Final Say

Standing at the front of a negotiation workshop of 100 professionals, I asked, "Who here has experienced a fail? And what did you learn from it?" While most of the room raised their hand, one woman in particular asked to share her story. Taking the microphone, she explained to us she had been working hard to raise her visibility in her organization, to show others that she was capable of doing more than the tasks in her current role.

A data-intensive project came up and needed a volunteer so she asked to lead it. Shakily, she said, she completed the project but was told later by the executive sponsor that she had made several errors.

Ouch.

Now, she could have quickly beelined from any data-heavy project in current or future existence, but after meeting about the issues with the executive, she did something different. (Something I'm not sure I would've been brave enough to do!)

She raised her hand *the very next time* a data project came up. This time, she led the project with her newfound knowledge and a resolve to get it right. Like a cherry on a sundae, her executive sponsor exclaimed afterwards, "She knocked it out of the park." In other words, she had succeeded!

As my workshop attendees started clapping excitedly for this woman, she closed with this: "So often, *you* get to write the end of the story." The tips that follow are meant to help you do just that:

- **Get curious.** No matter what kind of fail you experienced or "No" you received, who could you talk to to get more information or insight into the hurdle you want to clear? Or how could you query the decision makers in charge about what they'd like to see more of? Jodi Glickman, CEO of GreatOnTheJob.com, applied to Cornell's Johnson Graduate School of Management (JGSM) in hopes of earning a Park Leadership Fellowship, a $72,000 scholarship awarded over the two-year program. She got the news she was admitted to JGSM but was not offered the fellowship. She called the director of the program in hopes of lobbying for her candidacy, and started by asking questions to understand what criteria were used to pick candidates. It turned out the director hadn't seen her application because her GMAT score was below the threshold. But it was a program for leaders committed to community service and leadership—Jodi had been a Peace Corps volunteer and policy analyst at the EPA! After making her case, the director said, "How come I never saw your application?" The next day the director called Jodi to personally offer her the fellowship.

- **Make one more appeal.** If you truly care about whatever it is on the line—a job, a promotion, a denied acceptance into a program, or a stretch assignment, you'll be willing to go back one more time to show your persistence and dedication to it. Ask yourself, what's one way I could act today to request another meeting, a second look, an appealed decision, another try, or to alter my pitch and put it back in front of decision makers? Remember, their "No" is only final if you see it that way.

- **Avoid "Maybe. . ., I suppose. . ., and I guess. . ."** These mitigators weaken your position when trying to change someone's mind. Instead, advocate for yourself using strong, confident statements such as "I recommend. . .," "I propose. . .," "I'm requesting. . .," and "I'd like to see if you'd consider. . ." These small tweaks prompt people to take you more seriously. They illustrate your self-confidence in your idea and *yourself*. By speaking in clear, audible tones and using confident terms, you'll make it harder for them to say no.

Go ahead. Try another angle. Shoot your shot, even knowing you might not succeed. Nothing can take the place of persistence!

9 Scale Your Confidence

Gathered in a huge conference room, surrounded by a wall of windows and a beautiful city view, there was something extra special about this day at the office. There I was, celebrating a big win for the company I worked for—a massive new contract we'd brought in. The firm rolled out the red carpet too, with elegant jazz music playing, tons of yummy gourmet eats, and bubbling champagne (my favorite!)—not a normal feature at the office.

I mingled and mixed, feeling excitement about the good news and a little nervous, too, given the big crowd and big energy gathered together on this day. I made myself a heaping plate and poured some bubbly—then seeing a friend outside, I excitedly made for the balcony.

That's when I heard it. A loud "Thwap."

Right there, with everyone—including our CEO and leadership team in the mix, I had walked briskly—with purpose and momentum—into the glass wall. My food and champagne were dripping down the front of my pink dress and my face . . . well, it hurt!

All the air had exited my lungs. I felt like the most inept, disgraceful creature alive in that moment.

Later that day, as I iced my face at home, I felt certain that I'd never live this down. That everyone's eyes would bore into me when they saw me.

But then, a little, itty-bitty thought started to simmer in my mind. One that I couldn't help but latch onto.

What if no one cares?

Whoa!

Not just that, *what if some people do care—but I don't care about their reactions?*

Then, I added my favorite retort to my own self-consciousness (you'll recognize it from the last chapter). Shrugging, I said, "*So freaking what?*"

And you know what? That pie-in-the-face moment ended up being a turning point for me. Not just applied then and there in an embarrassing moment but as a lifelong skill. I know the learning behind it can help you too.

If you are going to develop your confidence—to really grow it exponentially, you need to embrace the idea that you will navigate life or learn lessons *with an audience watching*. Not just that, but it's time to make peace with the fact that you will fall on your face sometimes. It's not a question of "if," it's "when."

To scale your confidence, you need to take chances, move forward with imperfect information, and bet you will somehow work it out. Whether it's the graduate degree program you're interested in, asking a client to pay you the big bucks, stepping up to drive a new leadership initiative, or something else!

That means developing a healthy tolerance for learning on the go and making public mistakes. And you know what? That's going to require something important from you: a license to mess it up, to tolerate a "D+" here and there, to make a doozie of an error that might make you cringe. It requires you to rebel against your own self-consciousness. So be ready to briskly take yourself by the lapels and say, "I deserve a chance to learn and figure this out as much as anyone."

Scaling your confidence to new heights also means giving fewer hoots about what others think—caring less. That doesn't mean you don't value outside feedback or reactions, but you prioritize what the next right thing is *for you*, not them. Your number one VIP customer is you, and that's whose respect and opinion you put first.

Yeah, but what if they laugh?

You—and they—will forget it one day.

But what if they underestimate me—and I screw it up and end up proving them right?

You'll be gladder that you did it and learned from it, rather than avoid it.

And what if they see a weakness or vulnerability of mine and judge me or poke at it?

You'll be aware about your hot buttons and triggers for next time, and it will probably prickle less if and when you're set off.

We all have these what-ifs, but the idea is to eclipse them with the biggest what-if of all time: "What if I regret shrinking from this challenge? What if, on my deathbed, I think, 'Why didn't I trust myself more?!'"

I don't know about you, but that last possibility is simply not an option I want to live with. As you take risks and survive—strengthen yourself even—you can go bigger, bolder, and more audacious.

What you'll see is that sometimes even when your brain won't take the action you need, you can enlist your body, and it will be ready to serve. That'll often mean looking inside for answers to those big decisions, not assuming the right answer is *out there*.

Another important route to scaling your confidence comes down to owning your own story. As you'll see in this chapter, that means telling that story—from different angles—not just the pretty ones! Every time you do that, you give someone else permission to be real about their life, too.

You'll also learn about the mental, physical, and interpersonal ways to manage your energy and effort. That way, you avoid the conditions that most drain you, and instead, you'll find a cadence and flow that fuels you.

And what's the point of learning cool practices that help you build healthy self-respect if you can't pass them on? Get ready to spread the good by being a confidence mentor to someone who needs you. Right now.

The idea is to get to a place where—whether you're standing there in a stained outfit feeling like a dope or you're taking up space with pride and poise—*you know, like you know, like you know*, that your value, your worth, is not negotiable. No one has a claim on your confidence but you. So be your biggest raving fan. Know that great things are ahead for you. And then pity the fool who underestimates you.

Manage Your Energy, Not Your Time

The other day my nine-year-old daughter asked me, "What's it like to do your job?" I answered, "You know your computer for school? How it has an Internet browser on it? Well, being an entrepreneur and mom is like having 368 browsers open. At. The. Same. Exact. Time."

The scramble of life can feel like that for all of us. But there's an experience—a discovery—that helps me deal with that "browser madness." I learned it while I was working at Deloitte, where I was fortunate to help roll out a pilot program for employees on *managing your energy*.

I discovered that to really tune into my well-being and tend to my welfare and personal confidence, I needed to start noticing where I was spending energy. This is in contrast to what I was doing before: obsessing about where I was devoting time and trying to "3X" what I could accomplish in a given hour. Gah! Instantly, the focus on managing energy felt like a more gratifying, dignified pursuit.

You can benefit from this too! To start, consider these four aspects of energy management so you can take an active hand in shaping your life:

- **Emotional energy:** fueling positive emotions through appreciation, diffusing negative emotions, and looking at situations through new lenses.
  - ◆ Long lens: "How will I view this in six-month's time?"
  - ◆ Wide lens: "How can I take a broader view to get more insight and perspective?"

- ◆ Reverse lens: "How might the other person in this situation view this—and how might they be right?"
- ◆ Name one way you could fuel more positive emotions in your day-to-day (i.e. affirmations, uplifting books or meditations, coming up with counterstatements to negative thoughts) _____ _____.

- Physical energy: avoiding bodily energy drainers (for example, sedentary lifestyle, lack of sleep, alcohol use or overuse).
  - ◆ Pay attention to waning energy.
  - ◆ Fuel your body with smaller, more frequent wholesome meals and snacks.
  - ◆ Move your body with rigorous activity every day.
  - ◆ Take regular breaks for every 90 minutes of work.
  - ◆ Name one way you could feed your physical energy (i.e. daily walk, strength training, group or solo exercise) _____ _____.

- Mental energy: respecting your need to attend to intellectual tasks in ways that promote focus and minimize distraction.
  - ◆ Reduce technology interruptions when you need to focus deeply.
  - ◆ Prioritize your top goal for the next day and then focusing on that first thing in the morning.
  - ◆ Choose set times to answer emails and voicemails.
  - ◆ Name one way you could enhance your mental energy levels (i.e. creating distraction-free zones or periods, putting boundaries on social media usage,

negotiating the right conditions with your boss to do "deep focus" work) _____

_____.

- Spiritual energy: Fueling your fulfillment by pursuing activities that feel effortless and use your best gifts.

  - Uncover your why for spending your energy wisely.

  - Allocate time and energy to what you consider most important in your life.

  - Identify and live your core values in everyday ways.

  - Name your why for spending your energy wisely—why is that important to you specifically (i.e. having vigor left after work to be active with my kids, feeling lively enough to maintain and nurture my friend-ships, having enjoyable alone time, having sufficient energy to tune in to my partner)? _____

    _____

As you start to notice these quadrants of your life and where you're feeling energetic (or running on low batter-ies), you'll get better at putting less investment into things that don't matter. In my own life, while at Deloitte, I saw how I was giving all my juice to work and how I didn't have lots of oomph or patience left at the end of the workday for everything else. Guess what kind of mood that put me in at home? Yeah—not great! When you're spent, you might act crabby, overtired, grumpy, or apathetic.

The best thing about starting to notice your energy spend—and why it's important to you—is you become a much more active player in your everyday life. So promote the role you're playing. Your energy is the most valuable coin in your life. Remember to devote it to what matters.

Stop Breaking Promises to Yourself

I bet you've heard this before: "It's really important to keep your word."

Sure, who would disagree? But what if the person you break promises to most often is . . . *you*?

Case in point: I have been promising myself I'll clean out my basement for (if I'm being honest) *years* now. And I frown with disappointment every time I walk by the basement door.

How many times have you promised yourself you were going to work out, save money, or clean out the [fill in the blank]?

The truth is we've *all* broken promises like this, and it might feel like no big deal. After all, the only person you're letting down is you.

But failing to keep promises to yourself hurts your self-belief. Studies show that keeping promises holds a lot of emotional value—and when we break those agreements, there's a decline of trust.[1] Nobody wants that—or to feel an ongoing sense of failure.

Here's another way to look at it: breaking commitments is like having a flaky coworker. You're so used to them handing in work late or in an incomplete way, that you stop trusting them to do what they say.

Similarly, you hurt your *own* self-trust when you constantly flake on *yourself*. Author Scott H. Young says it best: "Breaking promises to yourself has the same costs as breaking it to other people.[2] Except the person you trust less is *you*." Boom!

Here's how you can move beyond superficial promises that never see the light of day.

- **Write it down.** If you make a promise and nobody heard it, did it really happen? The problem with making promises only in your mind is there's no trail, no accountability partner, no consequence when you fail to follow through. So, at a minimum, I'd like you to write your promise down, whether it's to sign up for a club, make plans to visit a friend, or research a different career. And then, I suggest you put it somewhere visible. You can make it even more conspicuous by sharing your commitment with a friend or relative who can ensure you're answerable to your promise.

- **Commit to less.** You wouldn't schedule an appointment with your doctor when you couldn't go. So don't overschedule yourself. Be hyper-realistic and pragmatic about what space you have to take on more. Then only commit if you're 90% sure you can meet it. That may mean reducing the size of your goal or commitment so it's more realistic. Or it may mean not committing in the first place if it's not achievable. Remember, less is more here.

- **Acknowledge that making good on promises is hard!** If you feel like you regularly bite off more than you can chew, you're not alone. It's a human tendency to want to think about future possibilities and dream big. But there's a reason most people don't keep their New Year's resolutions. By being one of the few who agrees to less and regularly follows through, you'll cultivate a healthy sense of self-respect, trust, and confidence. That way, when you say no to a new promise, you'll be saying yes to investing in the promises you've already made.

Your relationship with yourself is precious—don't undervalue it! Keeping your word to **you** is as important

as keeping your word to your boss, partner, or cherished friend.

Just remember, there's no competition. Focus on making small promises you know you can keep. The more you
prove to yourself that you are as good as your word, the
more confident you'll feel. And the more you can avoid
painful fails and setbacks.

Get Off the Hedonic Treadmill

On my desk is a blue furry monster with googly eyes. He's
not just cute—he's my daily reminder to make big, hairy,
audacious goals. When I was feeling particularly terrified
to propose an article to *Harvard Business Review*, a place
I'd only dreamed of publishing my writing, I looked at my
monster and smiled as I hit send on the email pitch. My
article was all about the importance of bringing stories into
the inclusion conversation—and I got to tell some of own
story in the piece. It meant *a lot*.

Finding out my coauthor and I got a "yes" was unforgettable. Just *wow*. Then, seeing the finished, published piece
was a whole other level of excitement!

Sounds great, right?

Not completely. Just one day after publication I found
myself thinking, "Okay, so what's next?" Here I'd felt like
I scored the winning three pointer in a game with my
article—but immediately after, I felt hollow. Out of habit,
the gears started turning, and my mind went to what
should happen next.

This experience, which lots of achiever types encounter, is called the hedonic treadmill.[3] It's a metaphor for the

human tendency to pursue one pleasure after another. To never feel quite satiated but to be in constant pursuit of chasing the next thing.

The thing about constantly looking for the next thing is that it actually threatens our well-being. After all, how can you stop and smell the roses *now* if you're obsessing about the next conquest? The great thing is that there's an antidote to the hedonic treadmill, and guess what? It's something that'll boost your confidence long term and your interpersonal relationships.

I'm talking about training yourself to savor positive experiences, which means paying attention to and appreciating positive events and moments. Savoring has a way of amplifying the good in our lives, and it's positively associated with higher levels of subjective well-being[4] and happiness[5]).

So how can you get off the hedonic treadmill and jump on the savoring train? Here are four ways to savor more of the good in your life:

- **Tell someone else about your win.** So often, others who care about us will point out an additional positive angle we didn't even see. Open yourself up to these moments by sharing what happened with those close to you.

- **Make a memory you can revisit.** Can you make a scrapbook page or mini collage about your win? Do it! It doesn't need to be Picasso level—not even close. The point is to savor your win as you create it and remind yourself of that good event later. I can practically guarantee future you will love looking back on your happy experience.

- **Appreciate someone who helped or was part of your win.** Sure, it feels nice to open a gift, but it's particularly awesome to give a needed one. Think of someone who helped with your win—maybe it's a partner or child, or an administrative assistant, mentor, or someone else. Tell them specifically how they contributed to your great turn of events. Then thank them.

- **Occupy it.** As your great news happens, let yourself get absorbed in it. Make a little mental layer or force field to keep it safe and protected so that killjoy news can't diminish it. To help with occupying and immersing yourself in your win, become more aware of how your body is feeling—what your thoughts are. This "tuning in" will help you mentally to slow down time and attend more fully to this good moment.

As you strengthen your ability to savor, you can do it more often than just *here and now*. You can reminisce too—savoring a wonderful memory or win that felt great in the past. To fully own the goodness of your successes, don't just learn to look up at the stars, ease in and watch them twinkle.

 ## Develop Your Anti-Goals

Is there a common work practice or norm that makes you roll your eyes in frustration? Something you can't stand? Maybe it's sitting in the same place all day, interacting with people only over a computer, or having back-to-back meetings all the time.

Or maybe it's something else?

The practice of developing anti-goals means deciding for yourself what exactly *you don't want in your career*. And it can be a powerful way to design a life that helps you actively avoid those things. It's a considerate, aware state that helps you build your energy and confidence.

So what am I talking about?

Some examples of anti-goals and solutions might be:

Anti-goal	Solution
Inability to do the deep work I thrive on	Designating certain days as meeting days and reserving others for deep work only
Feeling disengaged by a sterile, "bleh" home office environment	Creating an office space that reflects something about who you are and boosts your mood or energy
Checking social media compulsively over the weekend	Logging out of social media accounts Fridays at 5 p.m.
Doing the exact same tasks every day in a mind-numbing rhythm	Stacking tasks on each other with an eye toward variety and contrast
Responding to messages on your company's messaging app after work hours	Putting your notifications on silent or setting do not disturb hours

Take some time now to come up with a few anti-goals of your own. (Note: of course, not everyone has the privilege or power to redesign unappealing aspects of their job. This mindset is still important as you take on different roles and opportunities in your career, make career changes, or launch entrepreneurial pursuits.)

Anti-goal	Solution

In my case, when I got a deal to write this book,
I felt overjoyed. (Believe me, I went in and out of *terrified*,
too.) Even though a thousand happy thoughts flooded
my mind, an ugly one hit me hard. After being grounded
from traveling during the pandemic and leaning into
virtual work, I was starting to feel my body *becoming one
with my desk chair*. For over two years, I sat and I sat and
I sat some more. Aack . . . my body hated it. As great
as it was to get the news that "quick confidence" would
become real, writing the book sounded like the ultimate
sedentary project.

But noticing that chronic sitting felt like a red, blinking anti-goal to me, I decided to try something different.
I grabbed an old shelf from my basement and decided to
prop it on top of my home treadmill. I added a few books
to give it height—and secured my laptop on the stack.
And you know what? Even though I mostly walked at a
light, leisurely gambol—I wrote almost my entire book
from there!

Sometimes knowing what we can't stand—what we simply can't abide—without judgment, makes all the difference
in the world. Don't be afraid to "fire yourself" from the bad
stuff and grant yourself some understanding and slack. It
helps us find what gets us in the flow so we can accelerate
around challenges and curves. And it fuels our best ideas
and our confidence.

Instead of continually mustering your motivation to do what you don't want to do, make the choice to make a redesign or deletion. Sometimes the best way to grow is to subtract!

 ## Craft Your Key Leadership Stories

"I don't have any good stories!"

That's exactly what my coaching client said in frustrated resignation, while explaining that she wanted to get better at public speaking. She wanted to share more about herself with the team she managed, but nothing from her life felt meaningful, important, or *special* enough to make the cut.

Have you ever thought something similar?

The thing about stories is that they are the ultimate connector, across the span of your career. They help you to quickly build rapport, and they cement a really important truth—that you're *actually* human, that you have lived universal experiences that others can draw on or relate to.

Stories also build trust and help people see a different perspective. They can also reinforce a key message that others won't forget. In fact, in psychologist Jerome Bruner's book *Actual Minds, Possible Worlds,*[6] he argues that facts are 20 times more likely to be remembered if they're part of a story!

Peter Gruber, author of the best-selling book *Tell to Win,*[7] describes it this way, "Story isn't the icing on the cake, *it is* the cake." So how can you become more confident telling stories as part of your day-to-day? Start to see *yourself* as a storyteller by using the following skill-building techniques:

- **Identify the central message you want to convey:** As you get ready for an important moment where you could share a story, ask yourself, *What is really important for me to communicate today?* Usually, this is about the emotional impact we want to have. Maybe it's the need for clear, open communication. Or maybe it's a unifying rallying cry to have each other's backs—to actively help out teammates. Maybe it's a high-energy, motivating message to help people perform excellently as busy season approaches. Whatever it is, write it down now.

- **Mine your life for stories:** Now, taking the message you just wrote down, ask yourself and then answer at least one of these questions: "What's a time I learned a lesson about this? What's a surprise I encountered? What universal emotion arose for me (anticipation, nervousness, hope, fear)? How has my thinking on this evolved?" (Incidentally, pie-in-the-face, crucible, and against-all-odds stories are also really interesting to people.) Write down at least one answer to all of the questions I offered. You now have the starter pack to crafting a story.

- **Start logging your stories as they happen:** The best thing about telling more stories is that you get better at spotting them as they unfold. Did you just have a funny misunderstanding with your food delivery person or Uber driver? You can talk about that as you address the broader issue of clear communication. Or maybe you watched your child approach a tough challenge with diligence and patience; taking inspiration from that, you can share it with your team. Write these stories down—*anywhere*—the Notes app in your phone, in a searchable spreadsheet with tags, even in a shorthand on Post-its. You want to have them accessible when you need them.

The key here is to stop disqualifying your stories as *not-interesting enough*. For so long, as a speaker, I left out some of my personal stories, deeming them not quite worthy enough to be helpful to the audience. Yet when I told some of these tales to people one-on-one, they would comment, "That's a cool story!" So, slowly, I started telling more of my personal experiences in talks—and you know what? The door swung wide open to clicking more deeply with my audiences.

To develop true self-confidence, it's time to tell *your stories*. So go there! Talk about the mistake. Share about an aha moment that relates to your topic. Tell us how a leadership lesson from a personal part of your life can teach us something about your professional topic.

Make a connection like that, and you'll communicate, "You can trust me." You'll also grab your people's interest and deliver them something authentic and unexpected.

Ask Your Body to Do What Your Brain Won't

One of the more touching parts of watching *Frozen II* with my kids was seeing main character Anna navigate her own fear and pain. Here she thinks she's lost her sister and friend, realizing she can be eaten up by worry and despair in this moment, but she knows she needs to move forward. To survive in an uncertain world, as she says, she needs to "take a step . . . step again. It is all that I can." She realizes she doesn't need to know everything about the future to survive, she needs to just *do the next right thing*.

When you have your own moments of "Can I do it? Can I muster the strength or courage?" there's a way you can do the next right thing, too. It's by asking your body to do what your brain might not be ready to. So how does this work? Here are some examples:

Feeling nervous about inquiring or applying for a certain promotion? Ask your body to take the physical action of typing up an inquiry email to your boss and hitting send.

Thinking you embarrassed yourself in your last presentation? Ask your body to set a positive tone by walking into the next one with confidence and comfort. (I like to pretend I have a personal wind machine pointing at me, which helps me take long strides, put my shoulders back, and bring a little swagger!)

Dream of being considered for a certain award or accolade in your field? Ask your body to complete the application and hit "submit" (and to do no more).

Interested in making your first video for a social media effort but feeling shy and insecure? Ask your body to hit "record" on your phone and do Take One.

By drawing on the awesome capabilities of our bodies, we can swoop right over some of the analysis paralysis or overthinking that goes on in our minds. Now, we're not asking our bodies to do everything, mind you, but we're asking them to take over and do the next immediately helpful thing. That can help us beat decision fatigue and that awful feeling of stuck-ness!

What about you? What's something you'd really like to do but have been putting off or making excuses for? Write down two examples below, and for each one, come up with one or two bodily actions you could take. To. Start. The. Thing.

 Goal: _____. *Action I could ask my body to do:* _____.

 Goal: _____. *Action I could ask my body to do:* _____.

Now, go after your daring adventure. Start where you are with what you know today. It's time!

 ## Load up on a Growth Mindset

Sometimes a picture is worth 1,000 words. On my wall is a printed meme of a little orange kitten looking confidently into a large mirror. What does the kitten see in the reflection? A much larger, ferocious lion. (May we all be so fierce!)

Similarly, your own mindset and self-image can turbo-boost how you feel, leveling up your self-confidence. Or it can weigh you down like an anchor, keeping you tethered in place.

Now your own mindset might seem like a private thing, but I have news for you: it becomes pretty obvious pretty quickly what your outlook is like.

If it's positive and growth-oriented, you might venture a novel idea in a meeting. Or if you make a mistake, you might own it, lightly laugh about it, and move on. If you're working on a task you struggled with initially, you might tell yourself that you'll get more efficient with some time.

If it's negative and fixed, you might mitigate your speech or downplay your ideas. You might avoid challenging projects. You might disqualify yourself from a new opportunity out of a sense you can't do it.

You can probably see how one's mindset creates a self-fulfilling prophecy. The good news is you can actively steer your mindset in a growth-oriented direction. Try swapping out these thoughts and see what a strong self-image can do for you.

Fixed mindset:	Growth mindset:
"I'm not good at . . ."	"I'm working on . . ."
"I stick to what I know . . ."	"I like to try new things . . ."
"It's easy for him, he's a natural at it . . ."	"I'm going to figure out how he approaches it . . ."
"I'm either good at it or I'm not . . ."	"I can learn anything with practice and experimentation . . ."
"It turns out I suck at this . . ."	"I'm going to need to practice this . . ."
"I'm never going to get this . . ."	"What else can I try here?"

Think about it: every new challenge you take on can be a painful, humiliating reminder of your inexperience or newbie status. Or you can actively cultivate a mindset where you believe in the power of your brain, in the *power of learning*. Where you learn in real time.

If you find yourself making limiting absolutes, catch yourself. Decide you'll make a mental swap. Stop trying so hard not to lose face. Start saying the phrase "not yet"—as in, "I'm not client-facing/leading the team/writing the article/leading from the front *yet*." Let yourself goof some things up! As the researcher and author of the book *Mindset*, Dr. Carol Dweck says, "Love challenges, be intrigued by mistakes, enjoy effort, and keep on learning."[8]

Stop Looking Outside Yourself for Answers

Is this new job opportunity the right one for me? Should I make a geographic move and go for it? Should I ask my boss for what I really want?

With a maze of self-help and DIY personal improvement books out there, it's extremely tempting to think the right answers to our burning questions *are out there somewhere*.

Somehow, it seems like self-trust has been conditioned out of us.

But here's a shocker: none of "them"—the experts, our family members, the people in your network—know what's right for you *like you do*. It's time to really honor that fact. In one study, researchers devised a technique to measure intuition.[9] Using it, they found evidence that people can use their intuition to make faster, more accurate, and more confident decisions. Even the US Military is studying how a sixth sense and implicit learning can inform how soldiers adapt to new and challenging situations.[10]

To start tapping this reservoir of knowledge and experience, and to build your self-confidence in a lasting way, try experimenting with these techniques:

- **Rely on informed gut instinct.** The truth is, you will almost always be working with imperfect or incomplete information. Accept this reality. That way, you can use what you do have: your past experiences and observations—and your gut sense of what's right. Scan past events, experiences, and precedents you've observed for whether your decision is sound. You can ask, *based* *on what I know, what's the worst that can happen and what's the best that can happen?* Then check your gut instinct, or immediate sense of what's right. Together, this makes up your informed gut instinct.

- **Use distanced self-talk.** Dr. Ethan Kross, author of the bestselling book *Chatter: The Voice in Our Head and How to Harness It,* recommends using distanced self-talk to work through an issue.[11] Here, you purposefully shift into the third person when you speak. For example, I might say (using my nickname), "Seleens, I know this job offer feels like a big decision, but either way, you're going to learn and grow." Kross says this distanced, friendly self-talk is not only calming, it helps you make a better impression and improve your performance. It may also enable you to reframe what seems like an impossibility as a challenge. Can you say growth mindset?

- **Project into the future.** Rather than over-consulting wise outsiders, what if you appealed to the wisest, most knowing version of you? You know, your own inner Yoda! To do this, bring a question you're grappling with to mind. Next, see yourself in your mind's eye 10–15 years from now. What does *that person* have to say about the matter? Can they offer any perspective? Can they see something in the distance that's not front and center right now? With a job opportunity for example, they might encourage you to grow by trying something new rather than staying in your current role and doing more of the same. Essentially, when you're doing this, you're tapping your highest, most aware, experienced self to answer your own question. But it requires you to believe it's there in the first place.

Looking outside won't buy you the life you most want. Start today believing you can trust yourself. That right there is the path to learning how to live.

 ## Be Someone's Confidence Mentor

Picture someone who boosted your confidence. Did they challenge you to stretch what you could do? Vouch for your skills? Put an opportunity on your path that made a difference?

I can vividly remember a time when my confidence was boosted, and it made *all* the difference. I was an MBA student, and I was lucky enough to direct some of my own research. And I knew *just* what I wanted to do. Interview C-level women across industries to learn their biggest leadership lessons.

The problem: I didn't know a single woman in the C-suite, and I didn't have any connections to them either. *Uh-oh.*

The solution came unexpectedly: One of my professors at Johns Hopkins—Dr. Lindsay Thompson—said, "Selena, I'll approve your research on one condition: you have to go after the *giants*. Go after the women you *think* will say no."

Gulp. But that's exactly what I did. And you know what? *So many top-level women said yes*—30, to be exact! Those interviews transformed me, and I knew what I'd learned could help others. That research became my first book, which became my business and life's mission: helping rising leaders carve out paths to the top and helping organizations retain and engage their workforce.

Now I want you to think about this: *How can YOU "be a Lindsay"?* You can start with the practices here:

- **Be a PQA:** Great leaders don't just swoop in to solve an issue; they ask great questions so we can come to our own conclusions. To unlock that deeper level of thinking, be a perpetual question asker or PQA. Ask questions such as: What would it take for X success to happen? What conditions would need to be true to reach X outcome? How does X activity bring you closer to your goal or purpose? How could you think just a little bit bigger about your purpose?

- **Speak well of them:** Next time you're connecting two people, consider how you can make both individuals feel boosted and valued. What do you admire most about each of them? What are some accomplishments you can brag about on their behalf? Rather than saying, "This is Marcia from marketing," say, "Marcia brings great marketing leadership experience managing multiple campaigns just like this." Making networking or meeting introductions with this goal makes people feel appreciated, and they will remember you for it. Round up in how you speak about a person, and others' treatment of them will follow suit.

- **Have their back:** So often, behind every powerhouse is a team of people who have their back. Well, it's true for everyone, and *you* can be part of that team. Who do you see around you with high potential? What makes you think they're something special? Tell them! Better yet, share what you know about them with leadership, and/or encourage them to take action on their bold idea. And don't put it off—it's one thing to *think* about giving recognition where it's earned, it's another to *take action* before the thought leaves your mind.

Confidence mentoring means challenging and supporting someone—especially when they don't know they need it. With your outsider perspective, you're uniquely positioned to push them to reach higher and aim bigger. Teach them to make bold bets. Sometimes all it takes is your vote of confidence.

ENDNOTES

Chapter 1

1. Schiller D., Freeman J.B., Mitchell J.P., Uleman J.S., and Phelps E.A. (2009). "A neural mechanism of first impressions." *Nature Neuroscience.* 2009 Apr;12(4):508–514. doi: 10.1038/nn.2278. Epub 2009 Mar 8. PMID: 19270690.

2. Van Lange, P. A. M., and Columbus, S. (2021). "Vitamin S: Why Is Social Contact, Even with Strangers, So Important to Well-Being?" *Current Directions in Psychological Science*, 30(3), 267–273.

3. Epley, N., and Schroeder, J. (2014). "Mistakenly seeking solitude." *Journal of Experimental Psychology: General,* 143(5), 1980–1999.

4. Gunaydin, G., Oztekin, H., Karabulut, D.H., and Salman-Engin, S. (2021). "Minimal social interactions with strangers predict greater subjective well-being." *Journal of Happiness Studies: An Interdisciplinary Forum on Subjective Well-Being,* 22(4), 1839–1853.

5. Read, Daniel, and Grushka-Cockayne, Yael (2011). "The Similarity Heuristic." *Journal of Behavioral Decision Making*, 24(1): 23–46.

6. Cuddy, Amy, and Glick, Peter, and Beninger, Anna. (2011). "The dynamics of warmth and competence judgments, and their outcomes in organizations." *Research in Organizational Behavior*, 31, 73–98.

7. Zenger J., Folkman J. (2013). *I'm the Boss! Why Should I Care If You Like Me? Harvard Business Review online.* Retrieved on October 31, 2022, at: https://hbr.org/2013/05/im-the-boss-why-should-i-care.

8. Pascual, P. (2021). "How To Introduce Yourself Professionally: Follow These 3 Easy Steps." Talaera Blog: Business English Communication.

Retrieved on October 31, 2022, at: https://blog.talaera.com/introduce-yourself-professionally.

9. Creswell, J.D., Dutcher, J.M., Klein, W.M., Harris, P.R., and Levine, J.M. (2013). "Self-affirmation improves problem-solving under stress." *PLoS One*, 8(5):e62593.

10. Adam, H., and Galinsky, A. D. (2012). "Enclothed cognition." *Journal of Experimental Social Psychology*, 48(4): 918–925.

11. Thompson, D. (2022). "This Is What Happens When There Are Too Many Meetings." The Atlantic. Retrieved on October 31, 2022, at: https://www.theatlantic.com/newsletters/archive/2022/04/triple-peak-day-work-from-home/629457/.

12. Murdock, B. B., Jr. (1962). "The serial position effect of free recall." *Journal of Experimental Psychology*, 64(5): 482–488.

Chapter 2

1. Nair, S., Sagar, M., Sollers, J. 3rd, Consedine, N., and Broadbent, E. (2015). "Do slumped and upright postures affect stress responses? A randomized trial." *Health Psychol*, 34(6): 632–641.

2. Kille, D. R., Eibach, R. P., Wood, J. V., and Holmes, J. G. (2017). "Who can't take a compliment? The role of construal level and self-esteem in accepting positive feedback from close others." *Journal of Experimental Social Psychology*, 68, 40.

Chapter 3

1. Woolley, A.W., Chabris, C.F., Pentland, A., Hashmi, N., and Malone, T.W. (2010). "Evidence for a collective intelligence factor in the performance of human groups." *Science*, 330(6004): 686–688.

2. Tulshyan, R. (2018). "Women of Color Get Asked to Do More 'Office Housework.' Here's How They Can Say No." *Harvard Business Review*

(online). Retrieved on October 31, 2022, at: https://hbr.org/2018/04/
women-of-color-get-asked-to-do-more-office-housework-heres-how-
they-can-say-no.

Chapter 4

1. Nolen-Hoeksema, S., Wisco, B.E., and Lyubomirsky, S. (2008).
   "Rethinking Rumination." *Perspectives on Psychological Science*,
   3(5): 400–424.

2. Amabile, T. M., and Kramer, S. (2011). *The Progress Principle*. Harvard
   Business Review Press.

3. Mitchell, O. "Why your presentation shouldn't flow." Speaking About
   Presenting website. Retrieved on October 31, 2022, at: https://
   speakingaboutpresenting.com/content/presentation-shouldnt-flow/.

4. Acuff, J. (2017). *Finish: Give Yourself the Gift of Done*. New York:
   Portfolio.

5. Cirillo, F. (2017). "The Pomodoro Technique." Cirillo Company.
   Retrieved on October 31, 2022, at: https://francescocirillo.com/pages/
   pomodoro-technique.

Chapter 5

1. "The LARA Method for Managing Tense Talks." Stanford University
   SPARQTools. Retrieved on October 31, 2022, at: https://sparqtools
   .org/lara/.

2. Galinsky, A.D. (2004). "Should You Make the First Offer?"
   Negotiation, 7(7): 1–4.

3. Thorsteinson, T. (2011). "Initiating Salary Discussions With an
   Extreme Request: Anchoring Effects on Initial Salary Offers." *Journal of
   Applied Social Psychology*, 41(7): 1774–1792.

Chapter 6

1. Kang, S., and Tversky, B. (2016). "From hands to minds: Gestures promote understanding." *Cognitive Research* 1(1): 4.

Chapter 7

1. Levin, M. (2018). "Harvard Research Proves Toxic Employees Destroy Your Culture and Your Bottom Line." Inc. online. Retrieved on October 31, 2022, at: https://www.inc.com/marissa-levin/harvard-research-proves-toxic-employees-destroy-your-culture-your-bottom-line.html.

2. Dimitroff, S.J., Kardan, O., Necka, E.A., Decety, J., Berman, M.G., and Norman, G.J. (2017). "Physiological dynamics of stress contagion." *Scientific Reports*, 7(1): 6168.

3. Oberle, E., and Schonert-Reichl, K.A. (2016). "Stress contagion in the classroom? The link between classroom teacher burnout and morning cortisol in elementary school students." *Social Science & Medicine*, 159, 30–37.

4. Bradberry, T. "How Negativity and Complaining Literally Rot Your Brain." Talent Smart EQ online. Retrieved on October 31, 2022, at: https://www.talentsmarteq.com/articles/how-negativity-and-complaining-literally-rot-your-brain/.

5. Thaik, C. (2014). "Toxic Emotions Can Lead to Serious Health Problems." The Huffington Post. Retrieved on October 31, 2022, at: https://www.huffpost.com/entry/emotional-wellness_b_4612392.

6. Cook, G. (2013). "Why We Are Wired to Connect." Scientific American online. Retrieved on October 31, 2022, at: https://www.scientificamerican.com/article/why-we-are-wired-to-connect/.

Chapter 8

1. Willis, J. (2016). "The neuroscience behind stress and learning." Neuroscience online. Retrieved on October 31, 2022, at: https://

neurosciencecommunity.nature.com/posts/12735-the-neuroscience-
behind-stress-and-learning.

2. "Here's Your Worst Work Fears Come True, According
   To A New Survey." Press release online. Retrieved on
   October 31, 2022, at: https://swnsdigital.com/us/2017/10/
   heres-your-worst-work-fears-come-true-according-to-a-new-survey/.

3. "Forgiveness: Your Health Depends on It." Johns Hopkins
   Medicine online. Retrieved on October 31, 2022, at: https://www
   .hopkinsmedicine.org/health/wellness-and-prevention/forgiveness-
   your-health-depends-on-it#:~:text=Forgiveness%20is%20a%
   20choice%2C%20Swartz,better%20emotional%20and%20
   physical%20health.

Chapter 9

1. Calluso, C., Saulin, A., Baumgartner, T., and Knoch, D. (2018).
   "Distinct patterns of cognitive conflict dynamics in promise keepers
   and promise breakers." *Frontiers in Psychology*, 9, Article 939.

2. Young, Scott H., blog, https://www.scotthyoung.com/blog/2018/08/
   14/on-keeping-your-word/.

3. Brickman, P., and Campbell, D. T. (1971). "Hedonic relativism and
   planning the good society." In M. H. Appley (Ed.), *Adaptation-Level
   Theory*. New York: Academic Press.

4. Smith, J. L., and Bryant, F. B. (2017). "Savoring and well-being:
   Mapping the cognitive-emotional terrain of the happy mind." In
   M. D. Robinson and M. Eid (Eds.), *The Happy Mind: Cognitive
   Contributions to Well-Being* (pp. 139–156). Springer International
   Publishing/Springer Nature.

5. Jose, P., Lim, B., and Bryant, F. (2012). "Does savoring increase
   happiness? A daily diary study." *Journal of Positive Psychology,* 7(3):
   176–187. 10.1080/17439760.2012.671345.

6. Bruner, Jerome S. (1986). *Actual Minds, Possible Worlds*. Cambridge,
   MA: Harvard University Press.

7. Gruber, Peter (2011). *Tell to Win: Connect, Persuade, and Triumph with the Hidden Power of Story*. New York: Currency.

8. Dweck, Carol S. (2007). *Mindset: The New Psychology of Success*. New York: Ballantine Books.

9. Lufityanto, Galang, Donkin, Chris, and Pearson, Joel. (2014). "Measuring intuition: Unconscious emotional information boost decision-making accuracy and confidence." *Psychological Science*, 27 (5): 622–43. 10.1177/0956797616629403.

10. Live Science staff (2012). "US Military seeks sixth sense training." Retrieved on October 31, 2022, at: https://www.livescience.com/18850-military-sixth-sense-soldiers-intuition.html.

11. Kross, E. (2021). *Chatter: The Voice in Our Head, Why It Matters, and How to Harness It*. New York: Crown.

ACKNOWLEDGMENTS

Thanks to my family, especially Geoff, Leo, and Noelle, for keeping me company and giving me the loving nudges I needed to get this thing to the finish line. I also couldn't have done it without my super supportive mom and three big siblings. I owe many thanks to my Wiley editor Zach Schisgal and editorial assistant, Jozette Moses, for their belief in my idea and the doors they opened to make it happen.

The world is a better place thanks to people who challenge you to speak more clearly and boldly. Big thanks to my development editor, Julie Kerr, and managing editor, Michelle Hacker, for their perceptiveness and keen use of the red pen.

Boba Fett once said, "You can only get so far without a tribe." I owe a huge debt of gratitude to my tribe: Megan, Leslie, Mary, Anne, Kristin, Emily, Tanya, Nina, and Julie. I'd also like to thank Chelsea Wiersma, Jodi Glickman, Simone Ahuja, Madyn Singh, and Eva Jannotta for always, *always* having my back. Last, I'd like to thank Jennifer Bicknese for teaching me how to find the answers within myself.

ABOUT THE AUTHOR

Selena Rezvani is a recognized consultant, speaker, and author on leadership. She's coached and taught some of the brightest minds in business and has spoken at Microsoft, The World Bank, Under Armour, HP, Pfizer, Harvard University, Society of Women Engineers, and many others. She also consults to corporate management teams, using workplace culture assessments to help them be more inclusive.

Selena's the author of two leadership books: the bestseller *Pushback: How Smart Women Ask—and Stand Up—for What They Want* (Jossey-Bass, 2012) and *The Next Generation of Women Leaders* (Praeger, 2009). Selena's experience in leadership and career management makes her a frequent spokesperson and resource for news media. Her advice has been featured in *Harvard Business Review, The Los Angeles Times, The Wall Street Journal, Forbes,* Oprah.com, and ABC and NBC television. She was a regular commentator on NPR's syndicated *The 51% Perspective* and wrote an award-winning column on women and leadership for *The Washington Post.* In 2019, Selena's TEDx talk on gender bias was recognized with the Croly Journalism award. Today, she writes on leadership for NBC's *Know Your Value.*

Over the last three years, Selena's launched 25 popular online courses on LinkedIn Learning—which have

been viewed by over half a million learners. She has BS and
master of social work degrees from New York University
and has an MBA from Johns Hopkins University. Selena
lives in Philadelphia with her husband Geoff and 10-year
old boy/girl twins. For more information, visit: www
.selenarezvani.com.

AFTERWORD

One thing's for sure, NOW is a great time to invest in your self-confidence.

If you've been waiting to be a little more ready, a little more experienced, or a little braver, this is your sign to start now. NOW is the perfect time. . . to practice all the interpersonal, embodied, and mindset techniques I've shared with you.

There's something else I want you to remember: No one else is going to do it for you. No one's parachuting in. So commit to yourself.

As you do, make a point to bring that encouraging, friendly energy. Don't be harsh or unforgiving with yourself. Regularly praise and savor your own effort—you know, all the little ways you are trying to accomplish your goals and plans. Give yourself acknowledgment for having the courage to speak a little louder, to introduce yourself to a group first, or to share something that feels a little bit bold. It'll help you go further.

As you've learned in this book, when you commit to practicing self-confidence, you take control of your future. You begin to shape how you're known. You signal to the world, "I 400% belong here." And you don't just hope for things, you speak them into being. This life skill will grant more of your aspirations than you can dream up.

There you have it, changemakers! Now it's time to make this real. To put these skills into practice. To do some new experiments.

Reach out and connect with me on social media (@SelenaRezvani) and at my website, www.SelenaRezvani .com, too. That's where you find my latest coaching offerings and courses to fuel you up and build your leadership presence.

Your raw smarts got you here. Your ambition is powering you. This is your moment. Own it.

INDEX